William Jared Hall

The Slave Sculptor

William Jared Hall

The Slave Sculptor

ISBN/EAN: 9783744796217

Printed in Europe, USA, Canada, Australia, Japan

Cover: Foto ©ninafisch / pixelio.de

More available books at **www.hansebooks.com**

THE SLAVE SCULPTOR.

LONDON:
GEORGE ROUTLEDGE AND SONS,
THE BROADWAY, LUDGATE.

THE SLAVE SCULPTOR.

CHAPTER I.

THE AZTEC CAPITAL, AND ITS GREATEST BEAUTY.

PROBABLY no period of this continent's history, is of deeper interest to the American people, than that of the Aztec race, previous to and during the invasion and conquest of Mexico, by HERNANDO CORTEZ.

At that time great numbers in the Mexican capital and adjacent towns, were possessed of a knowledge of arts and sciences, and of mental qualities, which compared favorably with the Old World civilization. The great valley of Mexico was then one vast field of loveliness. The ancient capital was situated in the center, and surrounded by the crystal waters of Tezcuco; over which three grand causeways formed the only approach to the city, except by royal barges, or canoes of the natives.

This lake was interspersed with floating islands which rose and fell with the gentle undulation of the waves, and moved as by enchantment, over the waters. They were jubilant with the sweet notes of rare plumed songsters.

The streets, the squares, and, in fact, every available space in the capital, was adorned with trees and shrubs of the most luxuriant growth, and flowers grew everywhere. The atmosphere was ladened with delicious odor, arising from the myriad flower-beds, and was cooled by the spray of numerous fountains in the gardens, where they kept their ceaseless play amid statues, ornaments, and columns of polished porphyry.

This was the great Aztec capital. In certain portions of it, there were long vistas of low stone and mud houses, nearly concealed by the intermingling foliage of trees; while, in other sections, were gorgeous palaces, embosomed in forests of cypress, and surrounded with all the splendors of a not unrefined taste. Temples of the most magnificent structure arose at frequent intervals, and were marked even in the distance by their tall gilded spires.

Surrounded with all this grandeur, and apparent civilization, the mass of the people were, comparatively, semi-barbarians. Their monarchy was despotic. The will of the emperor was unquestioned, and his court was maintained with the most regal splendor; yet the monarch thought it no disgrace to assist, personally, in the inhuman service of the church.

Their religion was characterized with the most cruel barbarism. In the name of their idols, the lives of men, women, and children, were freely sacrificed in the most painful and revolting manner. Even the dead, thus slaughtered, were—in supposed command of these deities—made the subject of *cannibal feasts*, in which all classes appeared equally interested.

The stirring incidents of our story transpired during the period immediately preceding, and at the time of the invasion of that empire by Cortez; and while we seek to interest the reader in our story we shall present life pictures of the Aztecs as they were in the days of MONTEZUMA.

Conspicuous in that portion of the capital where the nobles resided, was a large palace, which stood in a thick forest of cypress, presenting an appearance of grandeur seldom witnessed. There were cool walks, sparkling fountains, and lakes swarming with gay-colored fish. The choicest flowers bloomed on every hand. Corridors with lattice screens, covered with sweet-scented honeysuckle, encircled the buildings. Balconies overlooked the ever-present park, and the turreted roof was verdant with foliage.

In the year 1519, this palace was the residence of .ord Ahuitzol—a descendant of a former Aztec king. He was over sixty years of age, a shrewd, intelligent man, whose presence and advice were considered of importance, and he was therefore, chosen one of Montezuma's confidential counselors.

Attached to his estate, were some two hundred slaves; yet his immediate family consisted only of himself, one son—

—Toluca—and an adopted daughter—Mazina—the former twenty-five, the latter twenty-one years of age. Lady Ahuitzol had been dead several years.

Mazina formerly was Ahuitzol's slave. When about one year old she was purchased of a man who came from the eastern coast. Though her skin at first was copper-hued, it had probably been colored, for it soon became clear and white. As she grew in years her form developed into exquisite proportion and beauty, and her mind betrayed unusual intelligence. She arrested the attention of Montezuma; who, interesting himself in her behalf, she became the adopted daughter of the old nobleman. She received marked favors from the emperor, and became a great favorite at his court.

It was a lovely evening in May, of the year named. The sun had just disappeared behind the western mountains when Mazina came from the palace for a stroll through the park. She was habited in the costume of ladies of her rank, consisting of four skirts, differing in length, and highly ornamented. Over these, was a loose robe of gaudy feather-work, decorated with gold work, pearls, emeralds, and *chalchivitl*—(a green stone of high estimation among the Aztics)—and fringed with gold lace and silver. The garment reached to the ground, and was held around the waist by a *maxltalt*, or sash of fine cotton texture, richly embroidered with feathers of the humming-bird, and bedecked with gold. Her arms were bare; though the robe fitted close around her neck. Her raven hair floated in luxuriant tresses over her shoulders, contrasting with her fair complexion, which did not exhibit one tinge of the dusky, cinnamon hue, peculiar to the features of the aborigines.

Mazina walked onward, with a queen-like tread; yet her gaze was downcast, and her countenance overspread with gloom. Following her came two female attendants, carrying wreaths of flowers, and cups of perfumery. She moved on over walks paved with polished porphyry, until she reached a bower in the farthest corner of the park. Dismissing her slaves, she entered the arbor, to find a seat within its retiracy.

Her mind appeared troubled, for she gave herself up to profound meditation. She sat there, till the shades of evening gathered into twilight—twilight into gloom. The rippling sound of a fountain near the arbor, had lulled her to repose Her hands lay carelessly upon her lap, and her head drooped forward upon her bosom. While thus unconscious, a short, thick-set man, with black robe, and black cowl or mask, that concealed his head and face, came cautiously toward the arbor.

Reaching the entrance he paused, watched the sleeper for a moment, listened to her breathing, then entered. Approaching close to her side, he knelt upon the stone floor, raised his mask, and gazed upon her features as best he could through the uncertain light. He then bowed his head, and, for a minute, appeared to weep. When his feelings had somewhat subsided, he removed from his bosom a curiously wrought locket, to which was attached a short gold chain, and clasped it around her neck. Then replacing the mask, he arose and walked quickly away. As he did so another person rose from a prostrate position not six feet distant, and gazed steadily upon the receding man, until he had entirely disappeared. Then he heard the dip of a paddle in the water of a porphyry-paved canal, which passed through the park, connecting the waters of an artificial lake with those of Tezcuco. He again crouched on the earth. Presently he detected the outlines of a man approaching, and immediately recognized the form to be that of Toluca—Ahuitzol's son. Grasping the hilt of his *itzli* knife, he crawled cautiously toward the arbor

CHAPTER II.

THE SLAVE SCULPTOR.

Two hours preceding this adventure by the arbor, in a large apartment of a low stone house, or shop, was a young man, some twenty-one years of age. In stature he was tall, and his form was athletically developed. His dress was that usually worn by the laboring class, showing clearly the outlines of his muscular frame. A close-fitting wrapper reached from his neck to his hips, leaving his arms bare to the shoulders. From his waist to the ankles, were wide, loose pants, held at the loins by a belt, and gathered at the bottom, On his feet were plain leather sandals, while a curiously wrought cap covered his head. A heavy mass of long dark hair fell over his shoulders. His face was evenly but strongly featured, while its expression was one of high intelligence, resolution, and tenderness combined.

This man was Maxtla Ytzcoalt—a renowned sculptor, who until eighteen years of age, had been a slave. At that age he managed to purchase his freedom, when, being possessed of the ingenuity of a sculptor, and possessing unusual powers of execution, he readily outstripped all competitors, and became a leading spirit among the members of his profession, which then numbered many artists of real greatness.

His workshop consisted of but two apartments. The front room which occupied the greater portion of the house was used as a studio, in which he was constantly employed. His business being the furnishing of ornaments for temples and dwellings of noblemen, gave him an intimate acquaintance with the ruling men of the priesthood, and an enviable position among the nobility, and his studio was proportioned to the patronage he received.

The rear apartment was that in which he slept, and he appeared to guard it closely. There was, apparently, but one entrance to the building, and that was in front.

Maxtla had concluded his day's work, and sat down by the door to rest. It was just in the dusk of evening, and he was thoughtfully watching the throng of citizens, passing and repassing along the street. At this moment, a short, compactly framed man, with a black mask and cloak, walked boldly into the studio, and cast a quick, furtive glance around. The sculptor recognized the man, as one whom he had often seen, and who appeared to manifest great interest in his behalf; yet he had never looked upon his face, for, upon all occasions it was closely masked. The long, sable robe at once revealed his holy office of priest. All such being privileged persons, their movements were unquestioned.

On this occasion he appeared agitated, and hastily remarked:—

"One you love is in danger. Enemies are plotting her ruin and yours. Be wary! Be cautious! or she will be snatched from you, and you fall beneath the sacrificial knife."

Maxtla sprang to his feet, and words of inquiry were trembling on his lips, but the door closed upon the receding form, almost ere they were pronounced. For a few moments Maxlta paced to and fro, his head bowed upon his breast.

"'Twas a strange affinity, he murmured to himself, that brought us together. She was a slave, so was I. Our past is beneath a cloud. A mystery encompasses our origin. We certainly are unlike those with whom we are surrounded. Is it this fact which draws us so closely together? Our hearts cling strangely to each other! Oh! Mazina, Mazina! I will hasten to your side, in this hour of danger!"

Throwing his *tilmalti*, or cloak, over his shoulders, he walked forth from the studio, securing the door after him.

A tall, slender form, enveloped in a plain black robe, his head covered with a heavy mass of long, coarse white hair, approached the rear of the building, and entered Maxlta's studio by a secret doorway, as the sculptor passed from sight, from the front door. Closing the small door quietly, the man removed from beneath his robe a curiously constructed light, which illumined the room sufficiently to observe distinctly such objects as were in it. The room was the sculptor's private apartment. On one side, in a reclining position, was a life-size statue in porphyry, of Montezuma. It was a noble piece of work, and the secret visitor appeared highly pleased while viewing it. The carving of the head and torso was all complete, and the lower limbs were roughly defined. After thoroughly examining the statue, the stranger disappeared by the secret door through which he had gained entrance.

Meanwhile Maxtla continued onward, and soon reached the great park surrounding Lord Ahuitzol's palace. He moved slowly forward, carefully scanning every object around him. Suddenly he detected the form of the priest who had visited him at his studio. He watched his movements until he saw him enter the arbor in the private park. Creeping noiselessly forward, Maxtla peered through the vines and beheld the priest kneeling in front of Mazina, who appeared to be asleep.

This singular movement startled the young man; yet knowing it would be death to interfere with a priest he tremblingly waited the result. How great was his relief, then, to see the cowled visitor leave the arbor, pass off across the park, and disappear! Maxlta then stepped forward, and was about to enter the bower when he heard the sound of dipping oars in the canal. He instantly crouched on the earth again. A moment more and Toluca Ahuitzol, with his long plumes and glittering robe, came stealthily toward the bower. Springing to his feet Maxtla exclaimed: "You cannot enter the arbor, Mazina is asleep, and does not wish to be disturbed."

Toluca, with a hoarse, taunting laugh, struck a powerful blow at the sculptor. Maxtla caught his arm and with apparent ease, sent him whizzing away, with such force as to bring him to the ground.

The astonished Toluca arose quickly, and hurried away toward the palace. These movements aroused Mazina from her slumber, and she came forth from the arbor.

"Why, Maxtla! you here? What has happened! Did I not hear angry words? I must have fallen asleep."

"'Twas nothing serious; but why are you thus tremulous?"

"Did I not hear the voice of Toluca?"

"He was here."

"Did you offend him?"

"I forbade his entering the arbor. He struck at me, and I hurled him away."

Mazina moved nearer the side of her companion, and in a low whisper, replied:

"I am sorry, for he is a desperate man."

"I do not fear him;" and there was a peculiar expression upon his features.

"Ah! Maxtla, you do not know what he may do. He has powerful friends, and may accomplish your ruin, perhaps, death."

At that moment they were interrupted. Three athletic men rushed precipitately into the arbor, and Maxtla heard the voice of Toluca, saying:

"Secure him, dead or alive! but do not harm the lady."

The sculptor sprang forward, grasped the right arm of the foremost assailant, and with a quick motion wrenched from his assailant's hand a heavy *maquahuitl*,* or sword. Then, throwing his left arm around the waist of the frightened Mazina, he raised her from the ground, dashed furiously upon his foes, and drove them all from the arbor.

Following up their retreat, Maxtla fought with the spirit of desperation. In the heat of the contest, the white-haired stranger, whom we saw at the sculptor's studio, appeared upon the scene, and with one stroke of his long spear, broke down the guard of the three assassins.

At this unexpected interruption the assailants fled, leaving Maxtla and Mazina with the mysterious personage. There appeared to be a magic influence in his presence, which inspired them with a feeling of awe; and, involuntarily, they stepped backward, before his keen searching glance. For one moment he stood leaning upon his spear; then slowly raised his left arm, stretched it out toward the palace, and with a significant gesture, motioned them away. Without a word, Maxlta and Mazina withdrew; when the white-haired stranger strode haughtily away.

Mazina sought her own room, where, throwing herself upon a couch, she lay tortured with painful reflections.

---

* The *maquahuitl* was a formidable weapon among the Aztecs. It was a two-handed staff, about three and a half feet in length, in which, at regular intervals, were inserted, transversely, sharp blades of *itztli*, a hard, vitreous mineral, capable of a keen edge, making a dangerous weapon, when skillfully handled.

The events of the evening had made a deep impression upon the Sculptor's mind, as he walked along the dark streets, he endeavored to fathom the probable result of his adventure. Reaching his studio, he entered by the secret passage; and for some time remained in a deep study in the darkness. At length procuring a light, he commenced working upon the statue.

CHAPTER III.

THE TWO VOWS.

Let us take the reader back a few hours previous to Mazina's leaving the palace for the arbor in the park. Lord Ahuitzol was seated in a spacious saloon of his palace. The apartment was commodious though not lofty. The ceiling was of odoriferous wood, ingeniously carved, and the floor was covered with mats of palm-leaf. The walls were hung with gorgeous draperies of feather-work, wrought in imitation of birds, insects, and flowers, with a curious art, and a glowing radiance of colors that presented a gorgeous appearance. Clouds of incense rose up from sensers, and diffused sweet odors through the apartment.

The old nobleman was reclining upon a cushioned seat, drawn up in front of an open casement, overlooking the park. A beautiful slave girl stood near him with a fan in one hand, and a bouquet of flowers in the other.

She was about twenty years of age, and was dressed in the style peculiar to serving maids in the aristocratic palaces of the Aztec nobles. Her form was small though symmetrically developed, and her features well molded. Her complexion was of a much, lighter shade than usual among the Aztecs. Her eyes were dark, keen, piercing. Her black, glossy hair hung in flowing masses, and reached to her waist. The expression of her countenance was agreeable; yet, a sly inkling of deceit lurked in the corners of her eyes, and an unflinching purpose lay asleep in her thin lips and flexible nostrils.

She was a singular person, possessed of a singular disposition. For her friends she would do any thing:—no sacrifice was too great to make for the object of her affection; while, for her enemies, no amount of hate or scorn was sufficient to appease her desire for revenge. Her name was *Meztli*

"Meztli, where is Toluca?" the old nobleman suddenly asked.

"My lord, I could not tell," replied the slave.

"Find him, and bid him to my presence."

Toluca entered the apartment, wearing the gay girdle and ample square cloak of the nation. It was a garment composed of the finest cotton, the four corners of which were gathered up around his neck. On his feet were sandals of soft-tanned leather, richly ornamented with gold. Both sandals and cloak were bedecked with feathers, pearls, and precious stones; conspicuous among which was the brilliant plumage of the humming-bird, surmounted with emerald and *chalchivitl*. Upon his head rested a *panche* of plumes, which floated gracefully down his back. With a proud, consequential air, the young man approached his father.

"Did you send for me?" he asked.

"I did, my son. Draw up a seat, and sit down. I would speak with you."

"I will listen," was the reply; and the speaker placed a low stool in front of his father.

"Have you seen any thing more of that strange black-robed priest?"

"Not lately," and the young man sat down on the stool.

"What do you think of him? Do you understand his movements?"

"I cannot imagine what he is after, or why he should be lurking around the palace."

"There is a mystery about this affair, and it must be looked into. Have you kept a close watch as I requested?"

"Yes, but I have detected nothing that would warrant any decisive steps. He frequently walks through the park, sometimes alone, then again in company with another priest, yet he never appears to notice any thing around him."

"Does he continue to wear the mask?"

"Yes, he always appears in the same sable disguise that he wore on the occasion of his strange interruption at the time we thought to rid ourselves of that plebeian sculptor."

"By the way, have you seen this Maxtla, lately?"

"Not since that particular occasion."

"I want you to take all the slaves you need, and bring that man to this palace. I have a place for him here, where he will be safe, and trouble us no more."

"I will take him the first opportunity, but he has powerful friends, and it would be madness to attempt his capture outside the park."

"Well, well; take your own course, but *bring* him *here!* That is my order. I will attend to him after he is once in the palace."

"Your command shall be obeyed. He stands too much in my way for me to remain inactive."

"Is Mazina less obstinate, since my last interviews with her?"

"Not a particle," and there was a sudden contracting of the muscles upon his face. "She asserts boldly that she *cannot* love me, and that she *will not* marry me."

"She *shall*, Toluca! or she shall feel the vengeance of my power. I will not allow the heartless ingrate to trample upon my authority. Toluca! she shall be your wife! I swear it!" and the old nobleman grew red in the face, as he gesticulated fiercely.

A low, suppressed laugh startled them. They searched the apartment; but discovered nothing near. After a short silence, during which they listened in vain for a repetition of the sound, Lord Ahuitzol continued:

"Go and say to Mazina, that I would see her."

"I will do so," and the young man left the saloon.

That moment Meztli glided cautiously away from under the open casement, disappeared among the shrubbery, and immediately entered the palace.

Toluca soon returned stating that Mazina was in the park, that she had dismissed her attendants at the bower. A flash of suspicion shot across his mind. He started suddenly as if some quick impulse moved him, and, without waiting his father's reply, hastily left the palace. Taking a slave with him, he was soon seated in a barge, gliding swiftly over the water of a narrow canal, toward the arbor.

The result of that expedition has been narrated.

The slaves fled precipitately, on the first appearance of the white-haired man, and even Toluca himself, could but wonder at the unexpected and efficient interruption.

Without visiting Lord Ahuitzol on his return, Toluca repaired directly to the eastern balcony of the palace, overlooking the park, in the direction of the scene, where seating himself in a thick bower of vines, he endeavored to ease his perturbed mind. At the same time he did not forget to keep a strict watch through the park, as far as his eyes could reach. Ere many moments he was startled by a light tread, and Meztli stood before him.

She leaned her arm familiarly upon his shoulder, bowed her head forward till her lips almost touched his cheek, then, in a low whisper, said:

"I thought you would be lonesome here alone, and I came to see you, Toluca. You used to ask me to accompany you, but now I am of little account. Your thoughts have turned toward another, and the old one has been cast away as worthless. Say, is it not so?"

The young man made an impatient gesture, yet, she quietly continued:

"Toluca, did you make those fair promises only for purposes of your own? Did you promise to give me my freedom, and make me your honored wife, when no such purpose was ever settled in your heart? I am not blind, Toluca; I see that which passes around me, and I *know* that you have deceived me. I have been faithful to you, and you have repaid it— how?"

"Have I promised any thing which I have not fulfilled? Away! you are my father's slave? Dare to speak to me again upon such a subject, and I will send you a victim to the insatiate gods of the *teocallis**"

Meztli sprang back; her face turned to a deathly pallor; yet, with a clear voice, she replied:—

"Farewell, Toluca, you have enjoyed my love; you shall experience my hate. I have no fears of the *teocallis*. The very moment you take that step, I will"—and leaning forward

---

* The Mexican temples—*teocallis*, "houses of God," as they were called—were very numerous. There were several hundred in the capital, many of them, doubtless, very humble edifices. They were composed of solid masses of earth, cased with brick, or stone, and in their form somewhat resembled the pyramidal structures of ancient Egypt. The bases of many of them were more than a hundred feet square, and they towered to a still greater height. The top was a broad area, on which were erected one or two towers. These frequently reached forty or fifty feet high, and contained the deities, and sacred images, to whom the sacrifices were made.—Prescott.

the whispered in his ear. He started like one stricken to the heart, sprang to his feet, and his countenance depicted the keenest anguish and horror.

Meztli watched these emotions with apparent satisfaction, and there was a wicked smile on her lips as she added:

"Yes, Toluca, you will curse the day that you were born, if you do not fulfill the promise you made me. I do not love you *now!* No! I *hate* the very ground you stand upon; yet I would have you bound to me—I would feel you in my power —would see you at my feet! Then—*then* base deceiver, will I spurn you as your deeds deserve. Away! I say. Away! from me forever!"

"Say, Meztli;" gasped Toluca. "Where, where did you learn—"

"Away!" she interrupted, with a haughty gesture. "I am your father's *slave*, as you have said," and her lip curled with a contemptuous msile, but dare to speak again, and I will whisper those mystic words in the hearing of our emperor. Then who will be most ikely to find their way to the *teocallis?*"

With a defiant expression, Meztli passed hurriedly away, and left Toluca to meditate at leisure.

The young nobleman paced to and fro upon the balcony, his arms folded, hisgaze downcast, his mind in a frenzied state. Presently he halted abruptly, struck his hand upon his brow, and muttered

"I have it. Cruzilli's dungeons are strong, and will be a fit place for both sculptor and slave. I will hasten and make the arrangement—prepare the apartments for their special benefit. Then we will see who has the most power to accomplish vengeance,—I or the minions in my way. Ha! Ha!" He evidently relished his wish, and immediately entered the palace. Soon he was passing across the park; his gay robe and plumes had been removed, and, in their stead, was a cap and a plain black cloak.

He continued his walk until he had reached a long distance from the palace, and was traversing a narrow, dismal street, in a less-frequented portion of the capital. Suddenly he paused in front of a large stone house, gazed cautiously around, then knocked upon the door.

"Who is there?" was questioned from within.

Three rataplan raps were given, when the door was immediately opened. Quickly entering, the door was reclosed and secured.

The warden of this grim place was a tall, muscular man, with a countenance indicative of brutal passions, yet the familiarity between him and the young nobleman appeared to be congenial and intimate.

"Well, my lord Ahuitzol!" exclaimed the man, when his visitor was seated. "To what enterprise am I indebted for this visit?"

"A glorious scheme, Cruzilli;" responded Toluca.

"So I suppose; but you are agitated! What's the matter? Had any trouble?"

"Yes, I have; and have work for you."

"That's good news; what can I do?"

"You know Maxtla, the sculptor?"

"I do."

"Could you get him into one of your dungeons?"

"Easily."

"He stands in my way—between me and the object of my affection. Do you understand?"

"I think I do."

"Will you prevent his troubling me again?"

"I will, my lord."

"Your pay shall be ample."

"I know who my friends are, and on whom I can call. Is that all I can do for you?"

"No! Do you know Meztli—father's favorite slave?"

"Can not say that I do."

"If she was pointed out to you, would you place her out of the way?"

"Yes, if it would serve you, by so doing."

"I would have her removed. She will cause me trouble."

"Then it shall be done."

CHAPTER IV.

THE SLAVE GIRL ON THE ALERT.

LEAVING these two villains, let us return to Metzli, and follow her, after she left the balcony.

Instead of entering the palace, as Toluca supposed, she passed entirely around the building, yet remained upon the balcony, and approached nearer to him without being detected In this close proximity, she listened to the audible words which he uttered, and watched him until he entered the palace. Then, with all possible dispatch, she descended to the park, secreting herself where she could watch his movements.

She dogged his steps to the stone house, marked the locality, and returned to the palace undetected. Gliding along the great hall, she ascended the grand staircase, and stood before the door leading into Mazina's apartment. Her features indicated acute suffering. Her limbs trembled, her breath was fitful, and she leaned against the wall for support. One moment only she hesitated; then her nerves appeared to recover. She cautiously opened the door. All was quiet. She leaned her head forward, and listened. She heard the gentle breathing of one in sleep; then cautiously entered. There lay Mazina upon her couch. Her pillow was wet with tears, and her cheeks were ashen-pale. One arm lay beneath her head, while the other lay across her bosom, as white as the rigid alabaster.

Meztli gazed upon the sleeper with a fixed purpose to wreak upon her some vengeance; for had not Mazina come between her and the man to whom she had given her very soul's life? But that sorrowful face disarmed her; and a low groan which then escaped Mazina's lips, sent a great pang of pity to the heart of the slave. Tears were in her eyes as she stole from the room.

Mazina awoke as the girl passed out. She seemed half conscious that some one had been bending over her, for she saw, in her vision, a guardian spirit which filled her breast with strength and hope as she became fully awake.

The locket upon her bosom attracted her attention. What was the curious thing? She had never before seen such an ornament upon any Aztec's breast. Where *did* it come from? she queried. Pressing its neck, up flew the lid, and then disclosed to her startled vision was an exquisitely painted face. It was of a woman; and oh, how like Mazina's own features! It was wondrous—as if it was her, as she would be, if years had added to her womanly graces. Verily it was a mystery. She kissed the bauble and wept over it—she knew not why.

While pondering over the experiences of the few preceding hours, she was summoned to an interview with the old Lord Ahuitzol.

Secreting the precious locket beneath her robe, she descended with a faltering step, to the apartments below.

She was self-possessed and calm—betraying nothing of the trying scene through which she had so lately passed. With wonderful power she concealed her emotions, deep down in her heart, bound there by a will and purpose unconquered.

As Mazina entered, the slave girl arose with a smile, advanced, sprinkled a few drops of sweet essence upon her head, and strewed a bouquet of flowers upon the floor, over which she would pass. She then caught Mazina's hand, knelt before her with the hand pressed to her lips, then arose, and conducted her to a seat, near the side of the old nobleman. She then returned to her stool, sat down, and commenced arranging another bouquet from a larger quantity of flowers, in one corner of the apartment.

"Meztli," sternly spoke the noble; "you can retire. When I require your services, I will send for you."

Indifferently the slave arose and passed from the room, only to crouch beneath an open casement where she could hear every word that passed between Lord Ahuitzol and his ward.

"Mazina, what about this young sculptor—Maxtla? Strange proceedings between you and him, have been reported to me. What does it all mean?" commenced the old noble, changing his position so as to face his ward.

"I do not know what you have heard;" she replied, timidly.

"Was Maxtla in the park, last evening?"

"He was."

"Did you hold any conversation with him?"

"I did."

"Of what were you speaking?"

Mazina's face crimsoned, and she hesitated.

Lord Ahuitzol did not affect to notice her embarrassment, and continued:

"I am acquainted with all the proceedings of that occasion, and I do assure you, it pains me to think that I have a ward thus ungrateful, when all the circumstances are considered."

"Indeed, my lord! I do not know what you mean;" and Mazina appeared greatly troubled.

"Then I will tell you in as few words as possible; you will then fully understand *your* position, and *my* desires. In the first place, you was my slave, afterward you became my daughter by adoption. This step was taken that you might be placed on a footing equal with my son; and thus an alliance between you and him could be effected. This ultimate event, was the sole object of my desires."

"I could not, indeed I *could* not *ever* love Toluca. He is so different from me. His disposition, sentiments, and, in fact, every feeling, are directly opposed to mine. I could *never* consent to such an alliance;" and Mazina began to weep.

"You *will!*" he exclaimed, quickly; flying into a fierce passion. "You *will* marry Toluca. That is settled. I give you my word, that you shall; and I mean what I say. Away! Leave me, ere I forget myself."

Mazina did not wait a second command. She left the saloon, immediately.

There was a smile and a frown upon Meztli's face, as she crawled cautiously away from the window.

Mazina ascended to the corridor, and walked onward, until she reached a secluded corner, screened by vines, which had clambered up the side of the palace. Here she sat down, and for a while gave free expression to her feelings, in a copious flood of tears.

She was completely screened from observation, by the thick intermingling foliage, with which she was surrounded.

As the calm succeeds the storm, so did Mazina's grief settle down into a quiet reverie, broken only by an occasional sob, the subsiding throes of an over-grieved heart. The past came up before her like a panorama, whose pictures were drawn from life. She saw herself, a child—a *slave*, compelled to perform menial service. She grew, her mind expanded, and reached out for something which it did not possess. There was a void in her heart, a feeling of doubt, of suspicion. In her dreams she fancied associations and scenes different from those around her, they were exciting, and made her heart bound with joy. From these dreams she awoke to the stern realities of her slave life. Years passed. The slave became a nobleman's daughter by adoption. With one step she had passed from poverty and toil to ease and distinction. Still, she was not happy. The change did not suffice to remove that feeling of oppression and isolation which had ever existed in her heart. It was a happiness to think of the playmate of her childhood, Maxtla. He was still a slave. Oh, how many hours of pure peace and joy had they enjoyed together! Their childish loves had given way to the more enduring affection of maturity, and this sentiment had grown with their growth, until their hearts beat like chords in harmony. In her prosperity, she did not forget him. He was struggling for his freedom, and she secretly aided him. With her assistance, he succeeded, became a free man, and renowned in his profession. *Now* what a sorrow was it which threatened her happiness and the life of one she held so dear!

She was startled from her reverie by the sound of footsteps approaching along the corridor. Toluca stood before her. A smile lit up his features, and, dropping upon one knee, he caught her hand, and pressed it fervently to his lips. She quickly withdrew it and started suddenly back. Her cheeks became pale, her eyelids quivered, and her heart sank within her.

"Dearest Mazina!" he exclaimed, his attitude that of the most humble supplicant. "Will you not listen to me? Can not you love me? Oh, speak that word, which would make me so happy!"

Mazina did not speak. She remained as a statue, while he continued:—

"Mazina, I have long loved you,—loved you with all my heart. I can not live without you. Say, dear Mazina, will you be mine?"

"That can not be," she replied. "You know ere you asked, what my answer must be. I have told you I can not be your wife. Why will you persecute me again?"

Toluca rose slowly to his feet. There was a glance in his wicked eye that filled her heart with fearful apprehension. There was no mistaking his hateful purpose of revenge and injury.

"You *shall* be mine!" he hissed, taking a step forward; "or you shall be ——"

"Hold! foul miscreant!" shouted a voice, hoarse with passion. "Flee for your life or I will hurl your vile carcass from the corridor. *Away!*"

The baffled villain turned, and beheld the strange priest, standing there like an avenger. Toluca fled precipitately, and his ears were saluted, as he hurried away, by the low, mocking laugh of Metzli, who had witnessed all.

CHAPTER V.

THE DOOM OF THE LOVERS.

WHILE these events were taking place on the corridor, at Lord Ahuitzol's palace, Maxtla Ytzcoatl was busily engaged in his studio. He had labored nearly all the previous night upon the statue, in his secret apartment, and was looking forward to an early day for its completion, when he would surprise the emperor with such an offering as no monarch before him had ever received. He was not aware that any person except himself knew of his undertaking; yet, it had been more than a year since he commenced the work.

The meridian of the day had arrived, still Maxtla was busily engaged. At that moment, a tall, ungainly, rough-featured individual entered the studio. The sculptor looked up, recognized the person and remarked:—

"Ah! Cruzilli, a pleasant day."

"Well, yes, rather. Got plenty of work now?"

"More than I can do."

"Sorry for that."

"Why?" and the sculptor scanned the features of his visitor, with a keen glance.

"Because I have work for you, myself;" the man replied coolly.

"Ah! perhaps I can do it. What's to be done?"

"You will have to accompany me to my residence in order to learn. The work will have to be performed there; and I am in a great hurry for it."

"How long will it take?"

"I could not say. Not long, I think."

"When do you want me?"

"This, or to-morrow evening you can come and see what I want, then do the work as soon as possible."

"I will come to-morrow evening."

"Very well, I shall expect you at dark."

"I will be there."

Cruzilli immediately left the studio, well pleased with his success; while Maxtla, unconscious of the villain's game, continued with his labor, his thoughts upon the fair Mazina. Until dusk he labored undisturbed, then walked forth, toward Lord Ahuitzol's palace.

Entering the park surrounding the home of his loved one, he moved slowly along beneath the tall cypresses, picking his way among thick shrubbery and vines, in the most secluded parts of the garden.

While passing through a cluster of intermingling foliage, he heard a low sob, and paused. Again he heard the sob, this time accompanied by a prolonged sigh. Pushing the bushes aside, he stepped forward into a small opening. It was quite dark, yet he saw the outlines of a woman. That it was her for whom he was seeking his heart told him.

"Mazina!"

"Maxtla! Oh, I am so glad that you have come!"

They were soon seated upon the grassy mound, from which Mazina had just arisen, when Maxtla asked anxiously:—

"Why this unusual sadness? You was not thus, until quite recently."

"No, Maxtla," was the low reply. "'Tis not natural for me to be sad; but my sorrows are more than I can endure."

She then related the substance of her interview with Lord Ahuitzol, and the threat of Toluea. Mazina appeared greatly agitated while relating the circumstances, and added:—

"I have but one friend at the palace."

"Who is that?" inquired Maxtla, his mind still upon the events which she had narrated.

"It is Meztli!"

"Ahuitzol's slave?"

"Yes; she appears to be very friendly. Were it not for her counsel and advice, I do not know what I should have done. I think she is good-hearted and loves me."

"I fear, Mazina, that you are deceived in her. Somehow I have taken a great dislike to her. I look upon her as possessed of a wicked heart; yet I hope I am mistaken."

"O, Maxlta! you are surely mistaken. There could no person be more kind to me than she has been."

"I trust you may not be deceived, yet I would caution you not to confide in her too far until you have thoroughly tested her fidelity."

"Maxtla! if we were alone, far away from these scenes, entirely alone—in a wilderness—in the mountains, anywhere, utterly alone—we should be happy. It seems that I have no friend in the world but you. All others are enemies;" and leaning her head against his shoulder, she gave way to her grief.

"We shall, dear Mazina," he replied, "some day realize the full extent of our hopes. We shall triumph over enemies, and O! Mazina, will we not be happy? For years we have struggled against fearful odds. We have been slaves together. Our past is a deep mystery, yet our hearts, from the first, appeared to draw toward each other by strong cords—sometimes they seemed stronger than mere love. Oh, that I could raise the vail from the past—that I could look back to our childhood—our infancy, yea, birth and parentage. I——"

A motion in the bushes interrupted them. The white-haired stranger stepped into the opening.

One moment his gaze rested upon the lovers; then quickly raising his right hand he pointed, with a significant motion toward the palace; a silent yet imperative command which caused Maxtla and Mazina to spring to their feet. The stranger passed on, and disappeared among the bushes.

Maxtla and his companion quickly left the retreat, and hurried toward the palace. As they passed along, Maxtla's quick eye detected the forms of three men, crouched on the earth close to where they had been seated; yet, not desiring needlessly to frighten his already trembling companion, the young man hurried forward, without communicating to her his discovery. Reaching the entrance to the palace, Maxtla bade her good night, promising to see her again on the following evening. He then passed off across the park toward his studio, little dreaming that he had parted with her for many a day of trial and torture,

As Mazina drew near the doorway, Meztli came running up, and, kissing her hand, requested her company to a short ride in a boat. It was early in the evening, and Mazina consented.

Meztli was expert with the oar, and loved to be on the water, while Mazina, having often accompanied her on similar expeditions, had no fears. They were soon gliding slowly down the canal, through the park, toward the wider channel which led into the open lake.

Meztli appeared in high spirits. Mazina was so amused that she forgot herself, and before she was aware of it they had passed from the channel, out upon the smooth waters of Tezcuco.

At that moment, another boat, bearing three men, was discovered pursuing them. Mazina became frightened, and urged immediate return, yet this might prove difficult, unless they could elude their pursuers.

Meztli appeared troubled, and pulled with all her might, yet kept the course of the boat directly toward the western coast of the lake.

On, on they went, swiftly over the water. The chase became exciting. Mazina trembled, and was fearfully alarmed, Meztli appeared to exert every muscle to outstrip her pursuers.

Ere long the boat shot high and dry upon the beach, when Meztli, catching Mazina by the hand, assisted her from the boat. Together they fled across the field. It was all to no purpose. They were speedily overtaken by their pursuers, and roughly seized. Resistance was useless; and Mazina, more dead than alive, was blindfolded, and her arms pinioned. Meztli was not so easily captured, yet she was eventually subdued, when they were conducted on across the fields, in a westerly direction.

Oh, for the presence of Maxtla! How the soul of the imprisoned girl cried out for his protecting arm as the ruffians bore her—she knew not whither.

"Maxtla! Maxtla!"

He, too, would mourn for himself as well as his last love.

At the appointed hour, Maxtla, unconscious of the misfortune that had befallen Mazina, started to fulfill his engagement with Cruzilli.

Reaching Cruzilli's residence, the sculptor was received with great cordiality, and was at once conducted to that portion of the edifice where the proposed work was to be executed. In a spacious apartment was a column of polished porphyry,

standing in the center of the room. Cruzilli represented that
he desired an ornament to rest upon this, and that it was to
be an eagle with spread wings, chiseled from a solid block of
jasper. Maxtla stepped forward to examine the block. Quick
as thought, like the breaking of glass, the floor parted from
under his feet, and down, down, into an abyss of darkness, the
sculptor passed. The floor closed with a significant crash
above him, and all was silent as the porphyry pillar, which
seemed to stand as a sentinel over that fiendish trap.

A feeling of dread and horror was followed by a quick stunning fall, when the victim became senseless. How long he
lay in that state, he could not determine. His first indications
of life were a sense of coldness, and a benumbed sensation of
his limbs. He next felt the floor where he lay to be wet and
slimy; and, with some difficulty, he succeeded in raising himself to a sitting posture.

At first he imagined himself to be blinded by a bandage
across the eyes. The impression was caused by a severe contusion on his head, occasioned by the fall and the impenetrable
gloom with which he was surrounded, and in which it was
impossible even to discover his own hand. A loathsome vapor,
like a heavy mist filled the dungeon; and which produced
a most nauseous sensation.

Quick upon the consciousness of these horrors came past incidents, and it did not require any deliberation to understand
that he was a prisoner—that he was, probably, where his eyes
never again would behold the blessed rays of the sun. His
doom evidently was sealed; the thought of it caused a cold
shudder to pass through his frame. Still he was not a man
to submit coolly. In the midst of the most appalling danger
his courage did not forsake him. He looked upon his situation as the triumph of enemies, whom he would foil, if possible. He sprang to his feet and glared around him, yet without
detecting a single object, so impenetrable was the darkness.
Sliding his foot along on the slippery floor, he moved cautiously
forward, for the purpose of finding the wall, and by sense of
feeling, to determine the dimensions of his surroundings.

His outstretched hand soon reached the wall, which, like the
floor, was cold and covered with a slimy substance—the accumulation of long years. He then proceeded carefully onward

eyes, and formal obeisance, they entered into the august presence of their sovereign; yet, in private, and to his immediate associates, he was condescending and social.

Three days subsequent to the disappearance of Maxtla, the emperor sat in a private saloon. With him was Lord Ahuitzol. The slaves had been dismissed. It was about the hour of four in the afternoon.

Montezuma was wrapped in an ample cloak of the finest cotton, beautifully embroidered, and his feet were incased in sandals of soft leather, all of which were bedecked with pearls, precious stones, and glittering with gold. His hair was black and straight, his beard thin, and his countenance paler than usual among his copper-colored race. In statue he was tall, slender, and well formed. He was, at that time, about forty years of age.

"Then you can find no trace of them?" he asked, continuing a previous conversation.

"Nothing, my lord, except what I have related;" replied the old nobleman.

"The movement appears to have been against both Mazina and Meztli; as I understand it?"

"Yes, Meztli was taken away with her, but the boat in which they were, was returned to the palace the same night."

"You think the abduction was effected through the agency of Maxtla, do you?" and the monarch looked steadily into the face of the old noble. "What reason have you for arriving at this conclusion?"

This was a somewhat difficult question to answer, yet, after a moment's delay, Lord Ahuitzol replied:

"For a long time I have noticed an undue intimacy existing between this sculptor and Mazina, and I have taken extra pains to express my disapproval of the course, on the ground of my son's prior claim. I think that they became discouraged of ultimate success, and he enticed her to leave the palace."

Montezuma did not reply immediately; he appeared to be in a deep study. Finally he rallied, and remarked:

"I will summon the sculptor, and enter into a speedy examination."

"I shall be grateful for your assistance in this, my hour of visitation, most noble sovereign;" continued Lord Ahuitzol, with apparent feeling. "Their recovery will restore to me a dutiful daughter, and a faithful slave. My son is inconsolable at his loss. He mourns deeply over the misfortune that has snatched from him his fair Mazina."

Lord Ahuitzol took his leave of the imperial palace, and Montezuma commenced pacing impatiently—to and fro.

"Yes! Yes! I *will* inquire into this affair!" and there was a significant expression upon his face as he spoke.

While the monarch was still promenading the apartment, the strange priest entered, unannounced. This was no uncommon occurrence. Montezuma had been a priest previous to his ascending the throne, and, it is said, that when his election was announced to him, he was found by the courier sweeping down the stairs in the great temple. Thus, it may be supposed, that a familiarity would be continued between him and the priesthood, which would be rigidly discountenanced with other subjects.

"Ah! good priest!" exclaimed the emperor; "I am glad that you have come. I need your aid."

"My lord has but to command," replied the priest reverently.

"I would have you seek Maxtla Ytzcoalt, the sculptor, and bid him hasten to my presence."

"My good lord," interrupted the priest; "it was of him I came to speak. He is missing, and there is suspicion of foul play against his life. I fear that the young man has been murdered."

"Murdered!" He started at the word, and then related to the priest the substance of his interview with Lord Ahnitzol. The priest listened attentively, and, in return, gave the monarch a partial account of his proceedings at and about the old noble's palace, during the past few days. He had haunted the place like a specter—for, was not Mazina's safety dearer to him than life?"

"I will accompany you to the sculptor's studio," exclaimed the emperor, after a moment's silence; "and will inquire into the particulars of this affair."

Soon the royal palanquin, blazing with burnished gold, emerged from the imperial court-yard, borne upon the should-ders of four nobles. Over it was a canopy of gaudy feather-work, powdered with jewels, and fringed with silver. In front of the royal chariot marched two aged officers of state, preceded by the strange priest in his sable robe and mask; while, on either side, and in the rear, were a crowd of young nobles who acted as a body-guard for the emperor.

Reaching the studio, the monarch descended from the litter, walked into the workshop, and his eyes swept around the apartment with a searching scrutiny. He then passed on to the rear room, leaning upon the arms of the two officers, and accompanied by the priest.

The old nobles uttered an exclamation of surprise, on beholding the wonderful likeness of their emperor, chiseled from solid block of porphyry. They were loud in their expressions of approbation of the remarkable powers of the sculptor.

Montezuma watched the movement and expression of his colleagues with a curious smile, and when they had become satisfied with examining the monument, he ordered that it should be carefully removed to his palace. The royal retinue then returned and entered the court-yard, amid the prostrate forms of the populace that had crowded around the procession.

The monarch soon issued a proclamation, which was published by heralds throughout the entire capital. The royal mandate announced that Maxtla Ytzcoatl had mysteriously disappeared, and under peculiar circumstances. Life, liberty, and power, would be the reward of any person, or persons, who would give information where the sculptor could be found, or that would lead to a detection of his abductors or assassins.

"Life, liberty, and power!" potent words for the ear of the slave or menial, who knew of these blessings only from their exercise by those who were his masters!

While the heralds were passing through the capital, crying the royal proclamation, Lord Ahuitzol was walking to and fro on the eastern corridor of his palace. His arms were folded, his gaze downcast, and his step firm and elastic. There was a lowering expression on his features, a close knit of the eye-brows, and a haughty grin upon his lips, as he moved forward and back among the clustering vines and thick foliage clambering about the corridor.

"Fool that I was," he muttered; "not to have foreseen this event; yet I will find her, if I have to scour every inch of the country, from coast to coast. I will offer great reward. I will have spies in every part of the nation. I will find her, and she shall marry Toluca. I will fulfill my oath, though it cost me my entire estate—yea, even my life; yet, any movement of compulsion if necessary to accomplish my object, must be concealed from the emperor. He must not know my designs. I will caution Toluca. He must be on his guard. This strange priest, I cannot understand him. He appears always near, and I believe he is leagued with that sculptor; yet all the information he gets will do him no good. Hark! what is that?" and he listened. It was the royal heralds, and his ear caught the words. They sent a thrill of satisfaction to his heart, and he became elated, even expressed his delight in a moderate laugh; well for his spirit of pride and spite that he did not comprehend the full import of the proclamation!

At that moment he was startled by the sound of footsteps. Looking up he beheld Meztli, her robe displaced, her hair disheveled, her features haggard and an expression of the deepest anguish on her countenance, as she came quickly forward, and fell prostrate before the old noble, weeping aloud.

Lord Ahuitzol was quite taken by surprise, but immediately recovered, and, stooping, assisted her to arise. She obeyed hesitatingly, and continued to weep, refusing to be comforted.

"O Mazina! Mazina! Where is she?" exclaimed the sorrowing girl, her face deluged with tears. "Has she returned?"

"No, Meztli," replied the noble; "she has not returned. Do you know where she is?"

"Me?" and she broke forth with renewed grief. "Oh, they tore her away from me, and took her to the mountains."

"Who did?" he questioned quickly.

"Alas! I do not know," and she continued to sob.

"Compose yourself, Meztli, and tell me all that occurred to you and Mazina after you left the park in that barge."

With considerable effort, Meztli related such incidents as the reader is already acquainted with, when she continued:

"We were both blindfolded, and so muffled as to prevent

our speaking aloud. Then, they immediately separated us, and took me one way, while they conveyed her another. I was taken to a deep cave in the mountains, and there kept until this morning, when I managed to escape, and came directly to the palace; yet I did not expect to find Mazina here, for I believe that she was taken away by those who intend to keep her safe."

Lord Ahuitzol immediately entered the palace. As he disappeared Meztli's grief suddenly changed to a wicked, triumphant smile; her lip curled contemptuously, and she cast a searching glance either way along the corridor.

"Thus far," she remarked, "I have succeeded, and my prospects are flattering. Mazina is safely disposed of for the present, and now for further conquests. Ha! ha! ha!" she laughed sneeringly; "they do not tamper with *me*, *I am a slave*—so he said, yet I have a mind to plan, a will to execute, with heart for revenge. I will bring that villain—Toluca, to my feet. He shall plead earnestly for mercy. What sound is that?" and she listened.

It was the royal heralds, and her ear caught every word.

"*Life*—LIBERTY, and POWER! to the informant!"

She glided from the corridor, descended to the park, and crept cautiously away from the palace, unconscious that she had left a dark figure, crouched on the roof, directly above where she had been standing.

She passed from the park and hurried forward with all possible speed. Ere long she stood in the royal ante-chamber, awaiting an audience with Montezuma.

CHAPTER VII.

THE SECRET CHAMBERS OF THE TEOCALLI.

The lake of Tezcuco, at that time, presented a scene of grandeur seldom equaled. Its clear, placid bosom was interspersed with floating islands, ladened with flowers, shrubs, and vegetation. These gardens originally were constructed of reeds, rushes, and other materials, knit or woven tightly together, until they formed a basis sufficient to support the sediment, which the natives drew up from the bottom of the lake. Gradually islands were thus formed, sometimes two or three hundred feet long, and, perhaps, one hundred wide, with a soil three or four feet deep. On these floating gardens the Aztecs raised vegetables and flowers for the great markets of *Tenochtitlan*—as the capital was then called.

Some of these islands were strong enough to support a hut in which a person, having charge of the island, lived, and with a long pole, he could change the position of his little territory at pleasure.

Approaching one of these larger islands on the afternoon, and about the same hour that Meztli returned to Lord Ahuitzol's palace from her reported captivity, was a light canoe in which sat Toluca.

Upon reaching the side of the island, he sprang out, secured his boat to a bush, and passed off toward a frail tenement, made of reeds and rushes.

In the entrance of this hut sat a woman, some forty years of age, whose singular appearance will induce us to pause for a word of explanation.

Her dark complexion appeared induced more from exposure to the scorching rays of a hot sun than from any tinge of blood. Her eyes were large, lustrous, and bright, and seemed not to have lost any of their youthful brilliancy. Her features were slightly wrinkled, yet bore marks of early comeliness. Her hair was black, long, and silky, through which were mixed a few scattering locks of white, and hung in loose, heavy masses upon her shoulders. Her brow was artfully sur mounted with a wreath of gay, sweet-scented flowers, and her robe was both picturesque and singular. It consisted of fine cotton, wrought with strange devices of birds, serpents, and insects, and bedecked with feathers, pearls, precious stones, and gold.

The garment reached from her neck to her feet, and was held around the waist by a belt of curious workmanship. Her arms were bare to the shoulders, colored with the juice of berries, and ornamented with bracelets of pearls and feathers. Her feet were incased in beautifully embroidered sandals, and in her hand was a long slender wand, wound with wreaths of flowers.

She was called Tonatiuh—the child of the sun. This sobriquet was given her on account of her miraculous power in telling future events. In short, she was a prophetess of great celebrity among the natives.

With her magic wand she professed to raise the dark pall, and look back into the most secret recesses of the past, or to lift the thick cloud that enshrouds the future, and read from the great book of destiny events yet to transpire.

"Ah! good Tonatiuh!" exclaimed the young noble; "I am glad to see you."

She arose to her feet as he spoke, leaned lightly upon her wand, and looked steadily into his face. Then slowly raised the magic stick, laid one end upon his head, and replied:

"The stars have spoken. Thou wouldst know of the past, and the future?"

"That was the object of my visit;" he answered, with a smile at her odd movement.

She did not affect to notice the expression, but with her head bowed forward, and her gaze fixed on the ground, she continued:

"I will speak as the stars move. Years ago lived a noble. He was great and good. He had a wife and son. The wife was meek and loving. The son was profligate and cruel, with a heart of steel. Eight years ago the wife—the bright star of the palace, died. The noble had a beautiful slave girl. He had many, but I speak of *one* in particular. She was sweet as the honeysuckle, and fair as the lily. The son showed great preference for her. She, in her artless simplicity, listened with an open heart to the oily words of the deceiver. She loved him—loved with all her young, innocent heart, led on by his promises and assurances of affection. She believed him and fell into his snare. Her life was forfeited—she saw the fate, which, according to the national custom, awaited her, and she trembled. The hideous gods of the *teocallis* were thirsting for her heart's blood as a *common sacrifice*—the penalty for her misdemeanor. He quaked with horror, for the *gladiatorial sacrifice* would be his punishment, did the emperor learn the facts. In an evil hour he concocted a hellish scheme. He took that young and still-confiding girl, and sunk her body in the lake. She was a slave, and but little was thought of her absence, while the son, supposing the deed was forever concealed from the eyes of the world, threw off the fear which had made his life accursed, and once again dashed into the gayeties of the imperial court. There was an eye, however, that had watched his movement. When the stone was tied to the weeping, praying victim's neck, and she cast into the water, a person who had also been a victim of the villain, was watching from a place of concealment, and saw the cruel act." While these words were being uttered, Toluca did not appear to breathe. He stood as a statue. His eyes fixed in a glassy stare upon the woman, his teeth set, his lips compressed, and his fingers pressed into the palms of his hands.

She continued:

"For a time, matters moved on smoothly, though he was nourishing a serpent in his bosom, which would, ere long, turn and sting him. He found another listening ear in another's love, less artless than the former, and quite his match in the art of revenge. While the seducer led her astray, she wound a coil around his heart till she could lead him at pleasure. By and by he endeavored to cast her off, and to turn his attention to still another victim. This one was the adopted daughter of the old noble—his father. She, however, had a lover, to whom her heart was plighted. She saw through the shallow mockery of his pretensions, and spurned him from her. He became angry—led his father to support his cause, and, thus armed, he laid violent siege to her heart. The cast-off slave, now revealed her power, and the villain trembled. He planned another scheme to entrap the slave and the favored lover. The lover was thrown into a dungeon, but the slave and the intended victim eluded the schemer's grasp. Shall I proceed further? Shall I lift the dark vail from the future, and read to *you!* that yet which is to come?"

"No! No!" he exclaimed wildly, and with a frantic gesture he rushed off toward his boat, and disappeared in it over the water, with a frenzied haste.

It was evening ere Toluca reached the park. Meztli with a smile, and a gay laugh came bounding forward to meet him. His first inclination was to pass without noticing her, but a new thought that instant entered his mind. Leading her to a seat, he questioned her relative to her captivity. With consummate artifice, she led him through such channels as she thought best, and framed such stories of her miraculous escape as would best suit her own purpose.

Any other than the half-frenzied eyes of Tolnca would have read in the maiden's face a subtle expression of satisfaction and revenge.

"Whom the gods would destroy they first make mad."

Toluca was mad!

Let us change the scene.

Upon a high eminence, called the hill of *Otoncaipolco*, in the chain of mountains on the west of the valley, and in full view of the great capital, was the huge *teocalli*, surrounded with ontworks of stone, covering an immense space.*

The period was the morning following the last scene between Meztli and Toluca.

In the eastern wall of the inclosure, overlooking the great valley, were two small apartments. These rooms were separated by an arch-doorway, across which was suspended a thick curtain of the finest texture and workmanship. It was embossed with feathers, fringed with gold, and hung with pearls; while precious stones, which formed no small portion of the ornaments, sparkled on the ample folds.

* "This memorable place is now indicated by a Christian church, dedicated to the Virgin, under the title of *Nuestra Senora de los Remedios*, whose miraculous image—the very same, it is said, brought over by the followers of Cortez—still extends her beneficent sway over the neighboring capital; and the traveler, who pauses within the precincts of the consecrated fane, may feel that he is standing on the spot made immortal by the refuge it afforded the conquerors in the hour of their deepest despondency."

Each apartment had a small aperture toward the east, through which the sun's rays penetrated, and during the day, furnished light and air. At night these openings were carefully darkened from within, that any light there would not be discovered from without.

The original purpose for which these apartments were constructed was not known, though it was supposed they were once the rendezvous of a band of robbers. Their existence was, beyond doubt, known only to the persons who then occupied them. The entrance was upon the outside of the inclosure, surrounding the teocalli, and a few feet from the base of the wall. It was a small cave of peculiar shape, and so furnished as to be comfortable for a place of abode.

Here, in this miniature cavern, two women resided. One was an elderly lady, who seldom left the cave, and who was constantly employed in ornamental embroidery, or featherpainting, in which she excelled. The other was Tonatiuh, the prophetess, who, in wandering about the capital and other places, pursuing her mystic calling, always carried with her a quantity of rich articles to dispose of among the nobles, and wealthy families. She owned a small canoe, and, while in the immediate vicinity of the city, made her home on the floating island where she had held the interview with Toluca.

No person entering this cave would have supposed, from appearances, that there was a passage leading to any apartments beyond. It was seldom that strangers called; but, when they did, there was never any thing visible to excite suspicion of other rooms and a more luxurious life.

A stone in the floor could be removed. It concealed an opening large enough to admit the passage of a person. Descending down into this, and passing along on a level for a short distance then ascending a long flight of stone steps, you would come to apartments in the wall, those to which we have referred.

These secret chambers were furnished in a style at once peculiar and sumptuous. The floors were covered with palm-leaves, the walls hung with draperies of feather-work, and the ceilings bedecked with rich hangings.

In one room was a couch, screened by the finest cotton, heavily embroidered, and fringed with gold tassels. From the center of either ceiling, hung a curiously wrought basket suspended by a silver cord, and holding a large *bouquet* of rich-scented flowers; while, scattered around in promiscuous heaps, were rare samples of the old lady's handiwork.

The sun had arisen but a short distance above the eastern mountains, visible far across the great valley, and was pouring its warm light upon the earth. Its rays penetrated into the opening of the cave, and fell partly upon the form of a woman, seated on a low projecting stone, engaged embroidering a large *tilmatli*, or cloak.

This woman was Meztli's mother. She had lived in this cave over twenty years. At the time she was married, her husband, with three associates, lived there, and used the secret chambers for various purposes.

It was there that Meztli was born, and when she was yet an infant, her father and his three colleagues were murdered by a marauding party from a neighboring tribe. This woman and her babe were then alone, and, for a few years, she struggled on in great poverty. Finally, she sold her child to Lord Ahuitzol, who supposed that the child's parents were dead. The mother had never visited the palace, nor had Meztli ever spoken of her as living, though, of late years, they had held frequent intercourse.

The mother was most skillful in embroidery and feather-painting—a branch of business in which the early Atecs excelled to a wonderful extent*

* How singular that such a beautiful art should have been allowed to perish! Cortez, at the period of his triumph in the capital, sent specimens of this work to Spain, where they elicited great attention, and were declared beyond the power of the most accomplished artists in the Old World to imitate. Their dyes were obtained from both mineral and vegetable substances, and their cloth was manufactured from cotton, raised in abundance through the warmer regions of the country. This important article was woven into any degree of fineness required, and, when desired, the web was colored with great brilliancy. They would also interweave with the fabric, the delicate hair of rabbits and other animals of like nature, and overlay it with representations of birds, flowers, and insects, making not only a warm but beautiful garment. Yet the art in which they most delighted, was *plumage*, or feather work, in which they could produce all the effects of the most perfect mosaic. The gorgeous plumage of the tropical birds afforded every variety of color and the fine down of the humming-bird supplied them with those soft aerial tints, which gave to their work that exquisite finish.

The worker at the cloak wore a melancholy countenance. She deemed herself alone, but even at that moment Tonatiuh came into the apartment. With a long-drawn breath, the Prophetess threw herself upon a seat, and remarked:

"I have had good luck, Tizoc. I have sold every article I took away."

The woman looked up with a faint smile, as much as to say she was pleased, then continued her weary task.

"I saw Meztli yesterday morning," Tonatiuh added; "and she told me that Mazina, Lord Ahuitzol's ward was in the secret chambers."

"She is," replied the woman without looking from her work. "Go up and see her, she is a sweet girl."

Tonatiuh started forward, and proceeded to descend through the opening in the floor, for the purpose of ascending to the chambers. Having reached the landing above, she moved the drapery carefully, and entered one of the apartments. Cautiously she stepped forward toward the bed and listened. Mazina was there and slept. Tonatiuh raised the gauze from the sleeper's face, and gazed steadily upon her features. One moment she bent over the slumbering form, then started back, dropped the gauze, pressed both hands upon her heart, and gasped for breath. She appeared greatly distressed, groaned audibly, while her lips quivered and her eyes filled with tears.

These emotions lasted but a brief moment. She again raised the gauze which concealed the white, clear features of the sleeper, and watched them closely.

"So like her," she whispered. "Those features. Oh, how often I have seen them in my dreams! but then, 'tis *only* a resemblance." That moment she caught a glimpse of the locket, half hidden beneath Mazina's robe. She took it in her hand, gazed at it, then opened it. Her features changed in an instant. The blood seemed all crowded upon her heart. Her lips were purple, her brain reeled, and she fell upon her knees with the exclamation: "O Merciful Father! I bless thee—I thank thee!"

CHAPTER VIII.

THE GLADIATORIAL SACRIFICE.

In one of the royal saloons were two persons—the emperor, and his nephew, Guatemozin. The young prince, Guatemozin, was about twenty-five years of age, and a great favorite with Montezuma. He was tall, slim, yet well formed; was shrewd, cunning, and brave, of good address, and well informed of what was going on through the capital. He was thus of inestimable value to the emperor as a friend, reporter, and counselor. They had been holding a long interview, and one of considerable interest, for Montezuma said:

"Take such assistance as you need, and remove every stone of the building, but find him and bring him to the palace."

"You shall be obeyed, my lord. I will find the sculptor, have no fears;" and the prince arose to depart.

"Stay, Guatemozin!" interrupted the emperor. "What do you think of those white strangers who are approaching the capital?"

"I think they would make good subjects for sacrifices;" and there was a significant smile on his fine features as he spoke.

"Well, hasten on your merciful mission," replied the monarch. "I have called the nobles and counselors to meet at the palace this afternoon, and determine whether we receive them as embassadors from their great king, or whether we sacrifice them to our gods."

With a formal obeisance the prince left the emperor, passed into the outer court, and was gone.

It had now been four days since Maxtla had been plunged into the horrors of that filthy dungeon, suffering all the agonies of thirst and hunger, and compelled to inhale the noxious and revolting effluvia of its portal of death. He had made every exertion in his power to effect an escape—as well might the tenant of the bottomless pit have hoped for release!

There was no means of deciding the length of time that he had been in the dungeon. It appeared an age of agonizing hours. Weak, exhausted, and discouraged, he crawled to one corner, crouched in a sitting posture, braced up by the walls, and there endeavored to become composed and reconciled to his fate.

If he could but have seen Mazina—if he could have pressed her to his heart, in a long, last farewell, he would have been more resigned. Even in his distress his soul longed for her, and her name trembled upon his lips like a prayer.

"Maxtla! Maxtla Ytzcoatl!"

Was it a voice from the gods? Had heaven opened to let in that gleam of light?

"Maxtla!"

He heard the call with the rapture that the earth must have felt when the day came out of the darkness. Yet he did not respond. He exerted every nerve, yet could not pronounce a single syllable! The perspiration stood thick upon his brow. He attempted to rise to his feet, but the muscles were powerless. Paralysis had taken hold upon his limbs.

"Maxtla! Maxtla!"

Oh, the horror! the agony of that moment! Would they close down the door, and leave him to die? or would they venture in to search?

Tears, the first that he had shed for many a day, gushed up from his heart, and rolled silently down his cheeks. In the hour of trial he stood firm. Death did not daunt him; but now that succor was near, yet might pass and leave him still in the noisome dungeon, was a thought too fearful for even his resolution.

Ah! his heart rebounds. A torch and a man are descending by a rope. The captive is blinded by the, to him, dazzling brilliancy of the dim light. His redemption had come! He heard a shout, wild and prolonged. A cold tremor passed over his heart, and he remembered no more.

Maxtla was drawn up apparently lifeless. Cruzilli stood near, and looked calmy upon the scene. Six of Montezuma's trusty generals, and prince Guatemozin, stood over that horrible pit, while, surrounding the building, were a thousand of the guard, awaiting the command of their leaders.

One word from Guatemozin, and the house would have been razed to the ground, yet he did not give the wished-for order. His hate was too great for any such vengeance, and Cruzilli was silently bound in strong cords for a torture his crime merited.

Maxtla was borne to a couch in a perfumed apartment of the imperial palace. A number of the most skillful medicine-men in the capital were summoned to his side, by command of the emperor. How low his lamp of life flickered in its socket, even these wise men did not guess.

Montezuma sat in a great audience saloon, surrounded by a number of his nobles and aged counselors. Before him stood Cruzilli, awaiting his sentence. The monster knew that he had nothing to hope for, and had firmly resolved to die without flinching.

The emperor listened with deep interest to the statement of Prince Guatemozin; and when he had concluded, the monarch ordered the criminal to be taken to the *Teocalli*, and there offered as a sacrifice upon the Gladiatorial Stone, to appease the god whose laws he had outraged. A fiendish smile lit up Cruzilli's features as he turned away, and, with a firm step, marched deliberately from the saloon under a strong guard.

The imperial mandate went forth, and in an hour's time a multitude had gathered upon the summit of the *Teocalli*. About eight feet from the wall, within the area of the great temple was a circular mass, perhaps three feet thick, resembling a huge millstone. To this stone Cruzilli was led by two priests, stripped to his waist, his head decorated with feathers, and his face painted with hideous devices. He was then placed upon the stone, bound to it by one foot, and armed with a heavy *maquahuitl* and shield.

In this position, and thus accoutered, he was compelled to battle against the attack of a soldier or officer, who was better prepared for the deadly encounter. If he should be overcome, he would be immediately conveyed to the altar of Common Sacrifice, and there butchered in a revolting manner. If he was not overcome, but successfully defeated seven consecutive combatants, he was then allowed to go free. Such was the law of the Gladiatorial Sacrifice.

As Cruzilli gazed upon the crowd gathered around him, his eye fell upon the features of Toluca. A smile passed over his countenance as of tumult as his grasp tightened upon the hilt of his weapon.

That moment an opponent stepped forward. His attire sparkled with jewels, and his weapons were of the most formidable kind. Cruzilli eyed him closely, apparently measuring the strength of his assailant, then quickly threw himself into an attitude of defense. It was plainly evident that he did not intend to be easily overcome, and it was very apparent that he was no novice in the use of the weapon which he held.

The officer struck the first blow. Cruzilli turned it aside with his shield, and brought down his own ponderous *maquahuitl* upon his adversary's head with such force as to cleave open the skull.

A wild shout went up from the assembly, when the writhing victim was dragged away, and another sprang eagerly forward; but it was impossible to stand before Cruzilli's awful blows.

One after the other of his opponents fell in rapid succession, until the seventh and most formidable adversary stood before him. Again his flashing eye swept over the assembly, and again that contemptuous smile passed over his countenance. The struggle lasted but a moment. Cruzilli's weapon descended with such crushing force as to break asunder his antagonist's shield, and scatter his brains upon the frail armor.

There went forth another prolonged shout, when the prisoner was released and borne in triumph from the *Teocalli*, upon the shoulders of the populace, who appeared equally satisfied with the slaying of seven, as if the one had been overcome, and his heart torn from his rocking breast to feed the insatiate gods.

CHAPTER IX.

FATHER AND SON.

WHILE these scenes were being enacted upon the *teoculli*, Montezuma was busy in his palace. He was sorely troubled, not only with the domestic affairs of his government, but there was a powerful and mysterious enemy marching steadily onward toward his capital, whose coming filled his heart with undefined terrors. Yet he maintained his outward composure, and dispatched a courier for Lord Ahuitzol and his slave Meztli. They immediately answered the royal summons, when the emperor, in consideration of services rendered by Meztli, who gave information where the sculptor could be found, rewarded her with freedom, and made her a privileged inmate of the imperial palace.

Lord Ahuitzol was then severely censured for his complicity in the intrigue, and peremptorily dismissed from the council halls. Toluca was condemned, and an order issued for his arrest.

These matters settled, their attention was turned to the all-absorbing interest of the period. The remainder of the day was devoted to discussing the course which they, as a great and mighty nation, ought to pursue toward the audacious strangers.

Montezuma was for peace. He favored the receiving of the bearded strangers as embassadors from the great king whom they represented. Prince Guatemozin bitterly opposed this course. He endeavored to convince the emperor that evil would come of the condescension, and urged that they stand up manfully and defend their homes and their temples from the pollution of strangers. The fiery and impetuous Guatemozin demanded that his sovereign should deputize him to remove the presumptuous invaders from the land, pledging his life, if thus empowered, to exterminate them in a week;

but the emperor ruled, and preparations were made to receive the Spaniards into the capital on the following day.

At this time—November 7th, 1519—the immortal Cortez and his little band of followers had gradually advanced from the coast, and now occupied the city of Iztapalapan, situated in full view of the great Aztec capital.

What think you were the feelings of that intrepid commander, as he gazed upon the long line of gilded edifices which reflected the rays of the setting sun in the dark blue waters of the lake? or looked around him and beheld the vast, almost innumerable hosts of natives, who, as he had abundant reason to know, regarded him with distrust and aversion?

As daylight faded, an almost impenetrable gloom spread over the scene. The hearts of Castile and Aragon beat wildly with solicitude for the morrow. Their peril never had been greater. The great capital, teeming with a population of hundreds of thousands, lay in quiet repose, apparently secure in its consciousness of superior numbers, and vast strength of fortification.

As the last vestige of light disappeared, the white-haired stranger emerged from the royal court-yard, and passed off toward Lord Ahuitzol's palace, to which place let us precede him by a few hours.

As Lord Ahuitzol, who, for so long a period had been one of Montezuma's most intimate friends, returned this time from the presence of his emperor, where he had been publicly dismissed, it may be supposed that his heart rankled with bitterness. Entering the park, he espied Toluca just returning from the scene on the *teocalli*. The old noble was so agitated and enraged at what had transpired that he could not speak; but he caught hold of his son's arm with a force that caused him to cringe.

Toluca in surprise followed his father, who led the way directly to a private apartment, to relate what had taken place at the imperial court.

"It is just what I expected," replied the young man as his father paused. "That priest-spy has been playing the eavesdropper, and has overheard our plans."

"Probably!" and the old noble appeared impressed with a new thought.

"I have determined upon my course," pursued Toluca. "Cruzilli is the leading spirit of a large band who have a stronghold in the mountains, and I intend to accompany him to their secret caves. Then I shall entrap that sculptor, and when he is once in my power, I will see that he does not escape. I shall trace out the hiding-place of Mazina, who, I believe, is concealed *by consent of the emperor*. When both are in my possession, I will have my own revenge."

"Your plan is good," replied Lord Ahuitzol. "I will remain in the palace, pretend to be indifferent to the emperor's displeasure, and assist you. When you have secured the game, I shall require your assistance. I do not intend to submit peaceably to such outrageous indignity; but of that hereafter."

"Yours to command," responded the son, elated with his prospects for his revenge; "but, there is one other person who stands in my way. I must have Meztli. She and I have a long account to settle, and those mountain caves will be a proper place to do it."

"When do you go?" inquired the old noble.

"Cruzilli will meet me in the park immediately after dark, when we will secretly leave the city, as it would be dangerous for him to be caught in the streets unless disguised. It was almost impossible to keep the stone-cutters from tearing him to pieces as he was brought down from the *teocalli*; and, but for the emperor's guards he would have been butchered."

The tireless, fearless, implacable Meztli arose from her knees. With her head bowed to the floor, and her ear close to the crevice beneath the door leading to the room where they were, she had listened to every word they had uttered. Nor was she the only listener. That mysterious priest had not been asleep, nor careless of the emperor's cause; for, as the treason-plotters ceased their conference, he glided carefully away from beneath a window of the apartment, and passed off across the park, in the direction of the great *teocalli*.

Toluca was busy until evening collecting and arranging

such articles as he desired to take with him into the mountain fastness. As nightfall came, he walked forth into the park to meet Cruzilli. Reaching the appointed place, he commenced pacing to and fro upon the edge of a canal until Cruzilli appeared, when the twain entered the previously provided boat, and moved rapidly off toward the lake. As they passed from the park into the main channel, that mysterious stranger, with the white hair, was standing, where he had watched them closely as they sailed within five feet of his place of concealment.

CHAPTER X.

THE SPANIARDS' ENTRY INTO THE CAPITAL.

As the first break of day became visible in the east, the Spanish General was astir, mustering his followers, who gathered around him with beating hearts. The sound of martial music awakened strange echoes through the valley and off among the mountains,—such as the natives had never before heard. The effect was wonderful, and the barbarians heard it with superstitious awe.

Far off across the lake, through the gray mist of morning, could be seen the sacred fires, ever burning upon the *teocallis*. Gradually the light advanced, until temple, tower, and palace were fully revealed in the glorious illumination of the morning sun as it overtopped the eastern barriers and poured over the beautiful valley a flood of glory.

The indomitable Cortez had marked his course from the coast with a succession of brilliant triumphs, such as had never before been achieved in the history of the world. A little handful of Spaniards, surrounded by myriad hosts, often threatened with entire annihilation, had marched on undaunted, unappalled, until now they gazed upon the capital of whose splendor they had been told. Though less than *four hundred* Spaniards, they marched forward. They beheld on either side, indications of wealth, power, and civilization. Although they had looked upon imposing scenery along their course, yet that encompassing the great capital was indescribably magnificent.

Entering on the southern dike (which was an immense construction of huge stones laid in cement, and wide enough for ten horsemen to ride abreast), they discovered that the lake was absolutely darkened by swarms of canoes, filled with Indians, who clambered up the side of the causeway, and gazed upon the strangers with curious astonishment.

APPEARANCE OF MONTEZUMA.

At the distance of half a league from the capital, was a solid wall across the causeway, called Fort Xoloc. Here the Spaniards were met by a large number of Aztec caciques, who had come out to announce the approach of the emperor and to welcome the white men to the capital.

After the usual ceremonies were concluded, the Spaniards followed their conductors toward the city; and, as they crossed a drawbridge, over an opening in the dike, they felt how truly they had committed themselves to the mercy of Montezuma, who, by destroying the bridges, could cut off their retreat.

Fears were not absent from their breasts when they beheld the glittering retinue of the emperor emerge from the great street which led through the heart of the capital. The monarch was bore in a palanquin of burnished gold, raised upon the shoulders of nobles, and shaded by a canopy of gorgeous feather-work, fringed with pendant drops of silver and shells.

When the train neared the Spaniards, it halted, and Montezuma descended from the litter, assisted by the lords of Tezcuco and Iztapalapan. As the monarch advanced, under a canopy held over him by young nobles, the obsequious attendants spread a cotton tapestry on the ground that the Imperial feet might not come in contact with the rude earth. His subjects, who lined either side of the causeway, bowed with humble reverence as he passed,—showing, by their attitude, the great respect which they entertained for their sovereign.

Montezuma was habited in a square *tilmatli*, or cloak, made of the finest cotton. His feet were cased in sandals, having soles of pure gold, while both the cloak and sandals were ornamented with feathers, pearls, and precious stones. On his head, held by a golden band of superb workmanship, was a *panache* of plumes of royal green, which waved gracefully over his shoulders. He was otherwise adorned with the greatest magnificence; and, as he moved along, the rays of the sun were reflected in ten thousand transparent brilliancies. His demeanor and bearing were courteous and condescending; and the meeting between him and Cortez was one of deep interest. At the close of the interview, however, the Indian monarch appointed his brother to conduct the illustrious strangers to the quarters prepared for them in the capital.

The emperor then ascended the litter and was borne away amid the prostrate forms of the populace, while Cortez resumed his march, and entered the city. Passing along its spacious streets, his wary eye studied the moving mass of Indians who thronged every unoccupied spot around the Spaniards; and well might he tremble, when he reflected, that did those natives but so determine, they could overpower him in an hour, and not leave one soul to relate the fool-hardy adventure.

The little band marched fearlessly into the heart of the great city, following their conductor. Finally they reached the old palace of Axayacatl, Montezuma's father, who built it fifty years before. The edifice was low, but commodious, and the apartments were of immense size, affording ample accommodations for the entire army. The court was surrounded by a formidable wall, in which the Spaniards found apparent security; yet the ever-watchful Cortez, planted his cannon, stationed his sentinels, and enforced the most strict discipline among his troops. After this disposition of his forces, the Spanish general was seated alone in a spacious saloon. He had been engaged writing a minute account of his entrance into the Aztec capital; but for a moment he had remained with his forehead leaning against the edge of the table, apparently in deep meditation.

Suddenly he became aware of a light tread on the floor. Looking up he beheld a short, thick-set man, completely enveloped in black cloth. In his cowl were two small round apertures, through which could be discovered bright, keen restless eyes. The man gazed searchingly around him as he advanced into the apartments. Cortez was not easily excited nor alarmed. His pistols and good sword lay on the table by the side of his writing, yet he made no effort to reach them. His gaze was fixed steadily upon his singular visitor.

One moment and the strange man drew from his bosom a heavy gold cross, set with four large diamonds, and held it up before the astonished Cortez. The Spaniard gazed first upon the cross, then upon the person who held it. The strange man watched the features of the general with a close scrutiny. He then replaced the cross in his bosom, drew forth a small piece of nicely tanned leather, presented it to the Spaniard, and immediately passed from the apartment through an ingeniously constructed doorway, which, until then, was unknown to Cortez. As this seeming apparition disappeared, Cortez glanced at the leather, and beheld characters written thereon in his own language. His eye ran quickly over the first line, and he sprang to his feet, while a sudden pallor overspread his features. The note read as follows:

"Most noble sir:—You and your little band of countrymen are in the most imminent danger. The people into whose country you have thus daringly penetrated, are treacherous, cunning, and cruel. They will offer you alms in one hand, and with the other, tear out your hearts to feed their heathen gods. I have watched your progress since you landed on the coast, with an interest of life and death. May the Virgin Mary and the Holy Cross protect you, and crown your efforts with success! Yet, I warn you to be vigilant. You have obtained access to the capital, contrary to the united voice of the populace, and all the leading lords of the realm, who are only held in restraint out of regard to their emperor—Montezuma, whom they have long honored and respected. One false move in you, or your generals, and your army would be overwhelmed by a legion of Aztecs. Then the blood of the Spaniards would flow like a river from the summit of the *teocallis*. Once again I urge you to exert the utmost watchfulness; and may God crown your enterprise with triumph!"

Cortez read this note carefully, two or three times, then folded his arms and commenced pacing to and fro in the apartment. A moment later, he summoned his little page—Orteguilla, and dispatched him to General Alvarado's quarters, with instructions for that officer to wait upon him immediately.

The attendant hurried away, and soon General Alvarado entered the presence of his superior officer. Cortez received him with that familiarity, which ever characterized his conduct toward his colleagues during that eventful campaign; and at once gave him the strange note to read. Following this, was a long, confidential conference, which resulted in a determination to double the sentinels, to enforce the most perfect obedience of the soldiers to their officers, and above all to command that a courteous, respectful demeanor, on every occasion, should be manifested toward the natives. Thus passed the first night of the Spaniards in the Aztec capital.

CHAPTER XI.

MAZINA AND THE PROPHETESS.

LET us now to the secret chambers in the wall, on the mountain, surrounding the Indian *teocalli*. The expression of Tonatiuh as she beheld the portrait in the locket, secured around Mazina's neck, awakened the slumbering captive, who sprang up, and gazed with amazement upon the woman kneeling by the side of the bed.

Tonatiuh's long hair, her head-dress of flowers, her rich costume, and, above all, her attitude, for a moment transfixed the attention of Mazina; then the consciousness that she was a captive, in a strange place, rushed upon her mind, and she cried:

"Where, oh, where am I? and *why* am I thus imprisoned?"

"You—you are with friends, fair lady," the woman answered, rising to her feet; and with a forced calmness continued: "But tell me, where did you get that locket?"

"If I tell you all I know of it, will you inform me why I was brought a captive to this place?"

"I will!" remarked the woman, quickly.

There was a deep earnestness in her tone, which Mazina interpreted favorably, and replied:

"One evening, not long since, I walked down into the park surrounding Lord Ahuitzol's palace, and shortly after sitting down in a bower, I fell asleep. It was probably placed around my neck, while I lay in this condition, yet by whom, or for what purpose, I can not say."

The woman then sat down on the edge of the bed, gazed searchingly into Mazina's features, and for several moments did not speak. Then rallying, yet appearing greatly agitated, she exclaimed:

"Answer me candidly a few questions. I am your friend, but there is a heavy load on my heart. The scenes of this morning have awakened old remembrances, which were fast sinking into an oblivion of forgetfulness. O God! I have suffered so much. My—my—" her head drooped upon her hands, tears gushed forth, and she sobbed like a child.

Mazina's heart was touched. This grief at once removed from her all feelings but those of sympathy; and, drawing near, she wound her arm around the woman's neck, pillowed her cheek upon her shoulder, and endeavored to console her with affectionate words.

As Mazina spoke, the fountains of her own heart broke forth, tears deluged her cheeks, and mingled with those of the strange woman.

Thus was the compact of friendship made between those two, whose future career was destined to be so closely interwoven.

When Tonatiuh had partially recovered, she took Mazina's hands, held them separately, gazed steadily in her face, and remarked:

"Have you a father and mother living?"

"Not that I know of," Mazina replied, with a slight tremor.

"Will you tell me how you came to be Lord Ahuitzol's ward? and what part of the country you came from?"

With the utmost confidence, Mazina proceeded to narrate all the early incidents of her eventful life, of which the reader has been made acquainted. She then, with childlike simplicity continued, and related the particulars of her intimacy with Maxtla Ytzcoatl, and the malignant opposition of Toluca, aided by Lord Ahuitzol.

During the recital, Tonatiuh listened with interest, and, after having questioned her closely upon the mysterious circumstances connected with the locket, to which Mazina could give no satisfactory answer, she said:

"I will now inform you, why you are detained here against your will; but, first, I would give you a short account of my mysterious manner of living. Ten years ago, I came first to this place, having journeyed from a city far to the southward. I soon became acquainted with Tizoc—the woman who owns or occupies the cave and these secret chambers; and I have since made my home with her.

"My profession is that of prophetess, which I adopted on

arriving here, for purposes of my own, knowing that it would allow me the most freedom to go and come without being questioned. I have, therefore, passed considerable time in the city, and have become acquainted with much that is going on in the great capital.

"I was informed by Meztli- Lord Ahuitzol's slave—of the friendship existing between you and the sculptor; and it was she who concocted the plan which effected your present captivity.

"Meztli, not so much from good will toward you, in thus placing you beyond the reach of those who sought your eternal ruin, as to serve her own purposes of revenge, succeeded in enticing you to accompany her on that evening boat-ride. Those men who followed in another bark, were hired to perform the work, and immediately after you was captured, she hurried on in advance to communicate with Tizoe, who is her mother. This woman started out immediately, and had proceeded but a short distance, when she met the men with you. They understood how to maneuver, and instantly fled, leaving you with her, when she conducted you to these chambers.

"As matters were at the palace, it was undoubtedly for your interest that the affair occurred as it has; for that villain Toluca, and his father, would have given you much trouble. Here you will be safe; but do not speak one word of what I have told you, for Tizoe is not any too well disposed toward you. I shall go to the city again in a few days, when I will see Maxtla, and arrange for a meeting between you and him; meanwhile, you must remain perfectly quiet. Trust implicitly in me, and I will effect your ultimate triumph. I must now leave you, but will return again soon. Do not part with that locket;" and before Mazina could make any reply, she was alone.

The morning which broke over the Spanish quarters, following their first night's sojourn in the Aztec capital, was very fair.

At an early hour, Cortez and several of his generals were seated upon a corridor of the palace where their troops were garrisoned, engaged in earnest conversation.

They had been there but a short period, when a woman

approached, bearing upon her arm a curious basket, filled with ornaments and jewels, which she presented to them, and made signs to purchase.

This woman we readily recognize by her robe, head-dress, and wand, to be Tonatiuh, the Prophetess. Cortez took a splendid necklace of pearls, and while he and his colleagues were admiring the superb workmanship, she was scanning their features with an earnest gaze.

The article was purchased by Cortez, who paid an insignificant price therefor, and immediately the woman passed off among the crowd and disappeared.

While Tonatiuh was in the Spanish quarters, Montezuma was seated in a private saloon of his palace. Before him stood Maxtla Ytzcoatl. They appeared to have been, for some time, engaged in conversation, for Montezuma spoke, continued:

"I want you to complete the statue as soon as you can. You will remain in the palace until it is finished, after which, I will make ample provisions for your future. The affairs of my government have become sadly disarranged since the white strangers appeared on the coast, and I can not tell what will come of their entering the city. For the present, I leave the entire management of the monument to you, and when the white invaders have returned to their own country, I will give my attention to a proper erection of it on the great *Teocalli*."

The sculptor, with an humble obeisance, retired from the presence of his emperor. As he was passing through the great hall, he met Tonatiuh, who had entered the palace.

"Ah! good mother!" he exclaimed, saluting her familiarly; "I am glad to meet you. Come to my room. I would ask a few questions."

Without a word she turned, followed through intricate passages, across open courts, among crowds of nobles and slaves, until they reached Maxtla's apartment.

"I know what you would say," she remarked, setting down her basket and seating herself. "You would know of Mazina —Where she is?"

Maxtla started and fixed a suspicious eye upon the woman; then suddenly recollecting that she was the noted prophetess—the far famed Tonatiuh, as the Aztecs called her, he replied:

"Yes, good mother, I would know of her. Can you tell me where she is?"

She sat a moment, her head drooped forward; then, without removing her gaze from the floor, she said:

"Mazina lives. She is in good spirits, and well cared for. If you would see her, meet me at the terminus of the western dike, this evening, at dark, and I will conduct you to her."

An exclamation of joy was trembling on Maxtla's lips; his countenance lit up with hope and satisfaction; when a courier entered the apartment, and announced that the emperor desired an immediate audience with the sculptor. The mandate was imperative, and reluctantly he obeyed, though not until he had assured Tonatiuh that he would be punctual to the appointment.

CHAPTER XII.

THE SEIZURE AND THE CAVE PRISON.

As the sun was slowly declining behind the western mountains, Maxtla went forth from the imperial palace, with a light heart and buoyant step. It had been three days since he was removed from the dungeon; in that time, he had recovered much of his wonted strength, yet was suffering from inhaling the noisome effluvia of that living grave.

Reaching the shore on the western border of the lake, it was quite dark. Tonatiuh soon approached, and silently beckoning him to follow, turned and led off toward the west.

Arriving at a convenient spot, in a thick cluster of shrubs, Tonatiuh requested her companion to remain concealed, while she went forward to conduct Mazina from her place of captivity.

Maxtla could scarcely wait for the promised return. Hope and joy filled his heart to overflowing. Absorbed in the thought of once again beholding her he loved, that he failed to detect a dark figure crawling on the ground toward the cluster of bushes in which he was secreted.

Soon the anxious lover espied the guide and her charge approaching. He sprang from the bush, bounded eagerly forward, and with a joyous exclamation, pressed to his heart the affectionate Mazina.

"Maxtla! O Maxtla!" was her only greeting.

Tonatiuh passed off into the darkness, leaving them alone.

For a few moments the lovers were silent. Then Maxtla heard a soft tread near him, and, on looking around, he received a blow which laid him prostrate on the earth.

Three leagues west of Tlacopan—a large city, situated at the terminus of the western causeway—was a wild country where mountains, steep precipices, and deep ravines, formed the scene.

Far down in one of these chasms was an opening, that led to subterranean chambers into which we must transport the reader.

The passage was small, and, to pass in, it was necessary to stoop slightly; but, having proceeded a few feet, the aperture was much larger, its craggy outlines, barely discernible in the dark shade, being illumined only by rays of sunlight which penetrated through the mouth of the cavity. The course was smooth, nearly level; and, after having advanced, perhaps fifty feet, opened into a cave of immense magnitude.

The space was enshrouded in total darkness, and the fall of a footstep, or the sound of a voice, echoed along the high vault with deep, unnatural hollowness. There was, apparently, no passage leading from this cave. Even had the dark, damp cavern been lit up with the light of noonday, no aperture would have been discovered; nor would the place have indicated that it was ever visited by human beings. The floor was covered with debris of rocks, and the walls presented a spectral yet picturesque appearance. Yet, upon approaching a certain place, and rapping twice upon what appeared to be a large stone, wedged in the wall, it rolled noiselessly back, and a faint light was discernible in the opening beyond.

Just within was a sentinel, who with his companions kept constant guard over this entrance. Having passed through this opening, the stone was rolled back by the sentinel, and then secured in a manner that would have resisted any force from without. Nothing short of pecking the stone to pieces would have moved it from its solid fastenings.

Having passed this formidable barrier, and traversed a circuitous route some thirty or forty feet farther, we reach another cave of nearly the same size as the former, though furnished in a manner more like some gilded apartment of the emperor's palace, than a subterranean abode, probably of outlaws.

There was no article of comfort or ornament enjoyed by any of the Aztec nobility, that was not to be found in this cavern. It was illumined with a soft pleasant light, and the atmosphere was ladened with delicious perfume.

From this cave were several passages, leading off in different directions, and communicating with other apartments; while one, which we will follow, lead over an intricate course of rough, loose stones, and through impenetrable gloom, for at least two hundred feet. Here, by turning an abrupt corner, we are ushered into a small cave, dimly lighted, and in which a sentinel guarded the passage not unlike that through which we first entered.

Having passed this, we continue some distance farther, when we emerge out upon a fertile valley, thickly overgrown with tall forest-trees, and low shrubs.

Early in the morning, subsequent to the interruption of the interview between Maxtla and Mazina, voices were heard near the cavern entrance. Soon Cruzilli and Toluca appeared in sight, and with them were Maxtla and Mazina. The arms of the couple were firmly pinioned, while they marched in front, assailed by the coarse jests of their captors. As they passed into the cavity, a small form glided over a cliff near by, bounded forward, and soon stood by the opening. It was Meztli. Her dark eyes flashed scorn and defiance as she gazed around with the evident intention of marking the locality. Then turning, she moved rapidly away, passed over the cliff and disappeared.

Reaching the sumptuous apartment of which we have spoken, Mazina was released by her captors. Overcome with fright and exhaustion, she sank helpless to the floor.

Maxtla's heart bled in pity for her sufferings. That moment his own hands were released, preparatory to having them more securely bound. With the rapidity of lightning, he slid from the grasp of his captors, and the next instant Cruzilli lay sprawling at full length on the floor, followed by Toluca, both having received blows that would have felled an ox. Then, stooping, Maxtla raised the frightened Mazina, and clasped her to his heart.

The two villains were soon on their feet again, and with fierce, menacing gestures, they advanced to the assault. Maxtla placing Mazina behind him retreated to the wall, and placed himself in an attitude of defence. His teeth were set, his lips compressed, his eyes flashed, and every nerve was concentraed for a desperate resistance. Toluca was not very strong, nor very courageous, and he purposely avoided coming within reach of the sculptor's arms. Cruzilli was more than Maxtla's equal in strength, yet not his match in science, and ere he had time to reflect, he lay quivering on the floor from another tremendous blow. Then springing forward, Maxtla made a pass at Toluca, which started the blood profusely, and he fell directly across the body of Cruzilli, who was just attempting to regain his feet.

As Toluca fell, Maxtla discovered a shield and *maquahuitl*, hanging against the wall. In an instant he sprang forward, grasped them with a smile of satisfaction, and stationed himself in front of Mazina, determined to defend her to the last. The two foiled villains arose with fiendish shouts, yet they were more wary, and did not needlessly expose themselves within the sculptor's reach. Toluca did not appear disposed to renew the attack, but exhibited a desire that Cruzilli should subdue the powerful opponent alone. Maxtla presented a defiant front, and he dared his captors to the battle. Cruzilli maddened by the taunt, and frenzied by defeat, armed himself with weapons similar to those of the sculptor, and with an air of confidence, he came boldly to the encounter.

Maxtla had moved away from the wall, where his club could have fair play. In a moment their weapons were whizzing in the air. Crash followed crash, in rapid succession. Neither faltered. They were equally matched, and the result appeared doubtful. Suddenly, Maxtla made a feint, then struck, yet his wily adversary recovered enough to parry off the blow, but it shivered his shield, and laid open one side of his head, tearing the scalp from the skull. He dropped the point of his weapon, staggered backward, then fell to the floor covered with blood.

Mazina fainted at the commencement of the struggle, and lay unconscious of what had transpired. At that moment, however, while Maxtla's attention was drawn toward the writhing Cruzilli, one of the sentinels, hearing the sound of battle, came stealthily upon the sculptor, and, with one full blow, struck him senseless.

Toluca, taking immediate advantage of the movement, sprang forward, and a moment later, the daring and dangerous captive was bound hand and foot. He was then conducted to a dungeon, where a heavy stone door closed upon him.

Mazina lay in an unconscious state upon the cold floor.

What of Tonatiuh?

Earnestly engaged with thoughts which seemed to absorb every feeling of her heart, she sat down at a distance beyond hearing of the lovers. Her head fell forward upon her hands, and her lips gave utterance to these words:—

"There is a mystery about her. She is unlike the rest of the people. Her complexion is so light, her hair so soft and silky, and her every movement so different. That locket! Who gave it to her? Who placed it around her neck? I must find the person! I *must* know where it was obtained. Hark!" and she listened. Her ear had caught a sound which for an instant startled her; but, hearing no repetition, she concluded that it was caused by some straggling person in the vicinity, and without giving it more thought, she gave herself up to her reflections.

In that deep meditation, time passed unheeded. It was some time before she aroused herself from the reverie. Then starting quickly, she hurried back to where she had left Maxtla and Mazina, but they were gone! She called, but there was no response. Was it possible that they had taken advantage of her generous absence, and fled? The thought troubled her exceedingly.

Little did she dream of what had really taken place!

CHAPTER XIII.

METZLI IN A NEW CHARACTER.

Thirty-six hours after the closing of the stone door upon the again-imprisoned sculptor, a singular person was seated on the ground, just outside the valley-opening of the cave. It was a young woman, apparently eighteen or twenty years of age. Her garments were such as were worn by the lowest class of people—coarse and ill-fitting. Her head was bare, her hair long, tangled, and of a reddish cast. Her complexion was a dark copper color, her eyelids drooped, and the expression of her countenance was vacant and half-idiotic. She had neither hat upon her head nor shoes upon her feet. Around her was a large collection of flowers which she had gathered, and from which she was forming a wreath, yet her work exhibited great awkwardness, and a woeful deficiency in taste.

While thus arranging her flowers, Toluca came from the entrance of the cave, but upon discovering her, started back, and, for several moments, watched her closely. Apparently satisfied with his scrutiny, he walked slowly toward the knoll on which she was seated. She failed to notice him until he had approached within a few feet of her, when, turning her head partly to one side, she eyed him with a bold stare, after which she arose to her feet and commenced gathering up her flowers. This accomplished, she marched off some distance, where she sat down again and began rearranging the flowers, without even looking back to ascertain whether he was following or not.

Toluca watched her for a few moments, then walked hurriedly up to where she sat and inquired:

"Would you like to work for good pay?"

She did not reply, but gave him another cold, indifferent side-glance, then continued her work. He was more earnest this time, and remarked:

"If you will go with me, and take care of a young lady, I will pay you well, and you shall be dressed as a waiting-maid of Montezuma's court."

"Where do you want me to go?" she asked, in a sharp, squeaking voice, letting her eyes glance over her shabby dress.

"I will show you, if you wish. The fact is, I was just starting out for the purpose of finding such a person as yourself, little dreaming that there was one so near."

"The work is not hard, and you will give me good clothes?" she questioned.

"Yes!"

"I will go and see. If I like, I can stay; if not, I can go, away."

"Certainly!" he replied, though his word belied his purposes. "You shall have easy work, and good pay."

Thereupon, she gathered up her flowers, and followed Toluca to the entrance of the cave. Here she refused to go any farther, asserting that the rocks would fall in and kill her; but, on being informed that a thousand persons lived in the mountain, she concluded to make the trial.

A few moments later, they stood in the apartment where the desperate encounter between Maxtla and Cruzilli took place. Here were forty or fifty men lying around, some talking and some sleeping.

Toluca, however, did not pause or exchange a word with them, but continued directly across the cave, entered an opening on the opposite side, and proceeded over a rough course for perhaps twenty feet, when he came suddenly into an apartment much smaller than the former, though it surpassed it in elegant furniture and hangings, and was illumined with a bright light. Here on a couch lay Mazina. She started as they entered, and exclaimed:

"Oh, tell me! is Maxtla dead? Do not keep me in suspense. Where is he?"

Toluca replied indirectly: "I have brought you a person who will assist in whatever you require. She will remain near you for the present, and I hope you will show more judgment for time to come, for you cannot escape me now. As for this sculptor of whom you make so much ado, I may as well tell you one time as another, that his life is forfeited by his own foolishness in opposing our purposes. No power can avert the fate which he has courted. If you are wise, you will exhibit less opposition to my commands, and show more respect for my wishes in time to come."

Mazina groaned in the anguish of her soul.

———

Four days passed—dismal, relentless days, in which the captive maid suffered untold agony. She wept almost incessantly. Weak, disheartened, and harrowed with the terrible suspense attending the fate of him she loved so well, her condition was deplorable. Toluca had been absent from the caves much of the time, and she was relieved of his detested presence.

Meanwhile, the simple waiting-maid remained close by the side of her mistress, and had succeeded in obtaining Mazina's confidence. She was kind, affectionate, and obliging, and the poor, persecuted girl found much comfort in the society of her faithful companion; yet the future was dark, drear, and threatening. How was she to escape the storm gathering over her head, which was intended to hurl her to destruction?—to crush her hopes, her life, all in the dust. The prospect would have made even a more courageous heart than hers tremble. Toluca kept a strict watch over her movements when he was present, and when absent he left a substitute.

Mazina's health failed so fast that it was thought advisable for her and her maid to walk out in the open air, morning and evening. At first Toluca accompanied them, then they were allowed to go alone, yet cautioned against venturing too far from the opening. Thus, a week passed by, and Mazina's health rapidly improved. Toluca was pleased, and encouraged the out-door exercise, little dreaming in what it would ultimately result.

During all these experiences, the waiting-maid, apparently not more than half-witted, performed her part in the drama in such a way as elicited the approbation of Toluca.

Ten days elapsed, and Mazina was quite well, or, at least, affected to be; and, one evening as she and her maid had walked some distance from the caves, they discovered a man standing upon a small hill near by

Mazina recognized him as being the priest, whom she had so often seen in the park surrounding Lord Ahuitzol's palace. With a smothered cry of joy she sprang forward, her heart swelling with the hope of deliverance. The waiting-maid turned and fled with precipitate haste toward the entrance of the caves, pausing ere she entered to look back and catch a glimpse of her mistress and the priest, as they passed hurriedly away to the east. An exulting expression lit up her features at the sight, but it vanished ere she reached the sentinel. A moment later she stood in the great cave. Here she listened attentively, and her eyes scanned the apartment with a close scrutiny. She then entered a narrow opening, and immediately stood within a small cavern enshrouded in total darkness.

"Maxtla Ytzcoatl!" she exclaimed.

"Has she escaped?" interrogated a voice which we recognize as the sculptor's.

"Yes, she left with a priest whom she appeared to know, and they are now on their way to the capital."

"Was he short? and did he wear a black robe and mask?"

"He did!"

"That is well," replied Maxtla, with apparent relief. "She could have fallen into no better hands. Is the way clear for me?"

"All but the sentinels and Cruzilli. The latter is not yet able to walk, while the others you will have to overcome by stratagem or force; and you must be lively, for Toluca, with a portion of his followers, will return soon. It is now just about sundown."

She had cut the ligaments from Maxtla's arms and legs, and directly the captive and rescuer were in the main cave—the scene of the desperate encounter between Maxtla and Cruzilli. Here the sculptor armed himself with a *maquahuitl* and shield, then turned toward the girl and remarked:

"I must thank you ere I go for your bravery and generosity in relieving my necessities, even in the face of danger and death. You have saved my life, and the life and honor of one who is dearer to me than my own existence. Without your thoughtful kindness I should now have been so reduced by want of sufficient nourishment as to have been perfectly helpless, perhaps dead. Why you, an entire stranger, should have taken an interest in *our* welfare, is more than I can say; but, sure it is that you have, and all I can now do is to express my gratitude in words. If you—"

"Come, come!" she interrupted impatiently. "Toluca and a score of his hounds will be here before you get away. You can overtake Mazina and her companion if you hurry. Turn square to the left as you emerge from the passage out, and keep straight ahead. It will take you directly to the capital."

While this colloquy was going on, the unsuspicious sentinel sat with his head bowed, nearly asleep. In this drowsy state a strong, violent hand was laid suddenly upon him, and, ere he could offer resistance, he was firmly bound.

In five minutes Maxtla had passed the formidable barrier, and was standing in the valley opposite the passage, and his eagle eye scanned the surrounding scenery with a close examination. The locality was new to him, but he remembered the directions given by his deliverer, and, without hesitancy, followed her instructions. He was soon bounding away from the caves, fleeing swiftly as a deer over the mountains.

He had not been gone many minutes, when the officious girl came to where the bound sentinel lay, and said:

"Tell, Toluca, when he comes, that his victims have flown; and you may ask him if he remembers Meztli? You can tell him also that her revenge is working bravely." Her scorn and dignified step betrayed to the eyes of the astonished sentinel another person than the half-idiot maid.

During all this period Tonatiuh was being tortured with severe trials. With all her ingenuity and craftiness, she could not unravel the mystery which surrounded that flight of Maxtla and Mazina, nor could she learn any tidings of them from that evening.

The third day after Mazina left the secret chambers, Tonatiuh returned from the capital and found Tizoc, the woman with whom she had lived nearly 'en years, dead! She had been murdered, and their little cave-home plundered of every thing worth carrying away; yet the assassins did not discover the secret passage that led to the chambers.

TONATIUH AND MAZINA.

Tonatiuh communicated the sad intelligence to the people of the *teocalli*, within the inclosure, and by them the unfortunate woman was buried. They took measures, also, to ascertain, if possible, who were the perpetrators of the fiendish act.

On the evening of Mazina's escape from the caves in company with the priest, Tonatiuh sat in the entrance of her now desolate home, brooding over the past. Her spirit was sorely depressed, and her cheeks were moistened with tears.

It was a lovely evening. The moon was at its full, and poured a flood of light upon the tropic landscape. The night-hawks screeched as they shot swiftly through the air the insects chirped among the bushes, and a delicious breeze moved the green foliage as it passed.

Tonatiuh sat there as the sun went down. She was there when the evening had far advanced, and when midnight came, she was still there. It had been a long, weary interval to her, and her heart had suffered during that period more than during years of her lifetime.

Suddenly she was aroused by coming steps. Looking out through the night she beheld Mazina rushing toward her. Tonatiuh sprang eagerly to her feet, and the next moment they were clasped in each other's arms, with a warmth and fervency that would have become mother and child.

"O mother!" sobbed Mazina. "You said I might call you mother. Do hide me from my enemies. I have suffered so much since I was taken from you!"

"Yes, child!" responded Tonatiuh, "you may call me mother, and I will find you a safe retreat; but tell me how all this has happened."

With simple, child-like confidence, Mazina related hastily the particulars of her and Maxtla's captivity, and of her escape through the assistance of a slave-girl and the priest; yet Maxtla was still a captive, and would probably die at the hands of his enemies; and she wept convulsively at the thought.

Tonatiuh consoled her with many words of encouragement, and, in turn, recited her own sad thoughts and experiences. "But the dear priest—where is he?" she exclaimed.

"I am here, good lady," he replied, stepping forward.

"Mazina is weary. She has traveled far and fast, and needs repose. Can you provide her with a safe place of concealment until I call again in a few days? She has told me of your previous kindness to her. Will you still continue to be her friend?"

"While I live, she has none better," Tonatiuh responded with much feeling. "Leave her with me. I pledge my life for her safety."

"It is enough! Be of good cheer, Mazina. I will bring you tidings of Maxtla, ere the sun has rose and set twice."

Maxtla Ytzcoatl flew over the mountain at the top of his speed. The full moon shone down in all its splendor, presenting to the eye a beautiful scene, spread out in the clear light.

While hurrying forward between two high rocks, he detected a moving shadow across his path. Looking up he beheld three men rushing down the steep declivity, directly upon him, and one glance revealed the foremost figure as being that of Toluca. In an instant the truth flashed upon the sculptor's mind that he had been pursued, overtaken, and now would have to fight if he would escape.

"Ah!" hissed Toluca, with a taunting voice, "you have not yet eluded my grasp. This hour is your last. You shall die, base slave that you are!"

"Not by your dastard hands!" responded Maxtla, armed with the *maquahuitl* and shield. "Let him who is in most haste to die make the first assault. Come on, villains, the whole of you!" he shouted.

With a sneering laugh, Toluca ordered his followers to aim their darts. One instant two cords were drawn back, till the *itztli*-pointed arrows rested against the full-strained bow, and the shafts poised for their fatal mission.

With perfect self-possession Maxtla threw his shield into use, and with the heavy *maquahuitl*, dashed furiously upon his foes. The onset was so unexpected, and the assault so terrific that the weapons were hurriedly discharged. One arrow missed him altogether, and the other bounded harmlessly away from the shield. A fierce sweep of the *maquahuitl* laid one of the assailants dead at the sculptor's feet, while the others retreated a few paces, then rallied, and came again to the attack. Maxtla well understood that his success depended upon instant action, for, did his foes once escape from the reach of his weapon, they could easily dispatch him with their arrows. Without giving his adversaries time to recover from the surprise of the assault, he brought another foe to the ground.

Toluca's previous knowledge of the sculptor's prowess had made him wary, and he purposely kept from the reach of his sword. The only hopes he had of success was with the arrows; but, unwittingly, he had brought his men too near, and the result we have seen.

As the second man fell, Toluca, with a curse, fled precipitately. At that instant his ears were saluted with a mocking laugh, and he beheld Mazina's waiting-maid, who was waving the branch of a tree in apparent triumph. Instead of the squealing voice of the half-witted fool, he heard the cool, menacing tones of Meztli, and her words quickened his pace into a frantic retreat.

CHAPTER XIV

THE GLORY OF THE "HALLS OF MONTEZUMA."

THE scene changes to the Spanish quarters in the Aztec capital. The period during which they had been in the city, was one of deep interest to them, and one also of eminent danger. They had, however, experienced nothing but the most friendly treatment from the emperor; still, the mind of Cortez was far from being at ease.

No one who has ever read of Montezuma's conduct toward the invading Spaniards on that memorable occasion, can fail to be impressed with his generous spirit, and more than barbarian manliness. To that very virtue did he owe the loss of his empire, for his Christian conqueror was a traitor of the most monstrous character. Montezuma lost his throne by too great trust in a Christian's word. Cortez won a throne by crime and treachery, which made even his age shudder. Had Montezuma possessed the fiery spirit of his brave nephew, Guatemozin, the Spaniards would never have entered the capital—certainly never would have left it, except in the smoke and ashes of the sacrificial altar, when their bodies were given to the flames.

Cortez's first movement on the morning following his triumphant entrance into the capital, was to pay a visit—by permission—to the imperial palace. On this occasion, he was accompanied by a band of tried followers, in whom he could place the most implicit confidence, and who were clad in burnished steel, with warlike accouterments of the most formidable kind.

They found the emperor seated in a spacious saloon, surrounded by a few of his favorite chiefs. He received the bearded strangers with the most marked respect.

Cortez, without needless delay, and perhaps without much ceremony, broached the subject nearest his heart. He was sensible of the vast advantage to be obtained, if the royal head could be converted to the Holy Catholic faith, thereby wielding a powerful influence toward the ultimate conversion of the Indians, and the present subjugation of the empire.

Montezuma listened attentively, until Cortez had concluded, when he replied, that he knew the Spaniard's God was a good one; but his gods were good enough for him. What his visitor had said about the creation of the world, was what he had been taught to believe. It was not worth while to discourse further of the matter.

The interview closed by the emperor distributing valuable presents among the Spaniards, who, notwithstanding their iron hearts as well as mail, were touched with the hospitality and kindness displayed by Montezuma.

Thoughts of quite a different nature, filled the mind of Cortez, who saw around him, the evidences of civilization, and consequent power. In the general appearance of the capital, its elegant architecture, its luxurious social accommodations, its activity in trade and mechanical skill, he beheld the enlarged resources of an old and opulent community, while, in the dense crowds that thronged the streets, were indications of an immense population, capable of vast revenues, if they could but be brought into subjection. He foresaw the importance of becoming perfectly acquainted with the capital, the character of its population, with the nature and amount of its resources, ere he could determine upon any final course of action. With this view, he asked permission of Montezuma to visit the principal public buildings.

The population of Tenochtitlan, or Mexico, was at that time, estimated at three hundred thousand souls, though it was probably much larger.

Cortez, having made himself familiar with the customs, habits, and forms of Montezuma's court; the great extent of his possessions; the sumptuous manner of his living; the homage paid him by his subjects; the pomp and grandeur of his entertainments; turned his attention to one of the most remarkable features in this semi-civilized city—the *Tianquez*, or great market. Here the Spaniards were astonished at what they beheld. The crowd of people pressing eagerly toward the market-square, was immense; and, on entering the grounds, Cortez and his followers' surprise was merged into amazement at the multitude assembled, the size of the inclosure, with the products and articles offered for sale. Every thing was in the most systematic order throughout the entire square. Officers were in continual attendance, whose business consisted in collecting the duties imposed on each huckster, regulating the measures, and bringing offenders to justice. A court of twelve judges sat in one part of the *tianquez*, whose extreme severity, in more instances than one, proved that they were rigid in maintenance of law. To every commodity was allotted its particular place. In one stall were bales of cotton, piled up in the raw material, or manufactured into dresses, articles of ornament and domestic use Another was assigned to a goldsmith, who made a good display of his ingenious collection. In another were specimens of pottery, vases, and trinkets of exquisite workmanship. In others, were hatchets made of copper, alloyed with tin—a fair substitute for iron. Casques curiously fashioned, representing different animals, and dyed with rich colors· the *escaupil* or quilted doublet, surmounted with feathers, pearls, and precious stones; arrows, lances, and the broad *maquahuitl.* There were also razors and mirrors made from *itztli*, which served the purpose of steel among that truly wonderful people.

There were booths in the square, occupied by barbers, who used the native razors in the performance of their vocation. Other shops were tenanted by apothecaries, well provided with drugs, roots, and other medicinal preparations. Conspicuous upon tables and shelves, were blank books or maps, for hieroglyphic picture writing. These articles are made of cotton, skins, or fibers of agave—the Aztec papyrus, and folded like a fan.

Everywhere, the eye met heaps of poultry, fruit, viands, and confectionaries. Cups of spicy, foaming *chocolatl* were set out on purpose to tempt the passer-by; while every stall and portico was ladened with rich flowers—the spontaneous growth of their luxuriant soil.

Thus, at one glance, did the Spaniards obtain a complete type of the industrial habits and resources of the nation, through the strolling visit to the great Aztec *tianquez.*

Their currency was a feature of much speculation among

the Spaniards. It consisted of small bits of tin, stamped with the letter T; bags of cacac; and transparent quills of gold dust. In all their dealings, it was a singular fact, that these people knew nothing of scales and weights. They were invariably governed by measures and numbers.

From this bustling scene, the Spaniards turned their attention to the great pyramid. It was situated in a vast area, encompassed by a wall, which was ornamented on the outside, with representations of serpents cut in relief, and which gave it the name of *coatepantli*—" Wall of the Serpents."

When Cortez arrived at the base of the pyramid, he found the emperor in his litter, waiting the Spanish general's arrival. Two priests, and several Aztec chiefs, by command of Montezuma, then stepped forward to raise the general upon their shoulders, and carry him to the summit; but Cortez declined the compliment, and placing himself at the head of his followers, marched boldly up the ascent.

Having reached the top, a magnificent view was presented. He could discover the great metropolis, at one sweeping glance, around which lay the clear waters of Tezcuco. The Spanish soldiers were filled with admiration, and spoke openly of the grandeur of the work. Far off, in an unbroken line, they could behold the base of that great range of mountains, surrounding the valley, and their icy summits glittered in the bright sunlight.

Having indulged in the grand spectacle, until they were satisfied, Cortez asked permission to enter the temples and examine the shrines of their gods. To this, Montezuma, after a short consultation with the priests, consented; and, in person, he escorted the Spaniards into their sacred sanctuaries—there being two on the pyramid.

The first entered, was a large, gilded apartment, and before the altar stood the statue of *Huitzilopotchli*—the war-god of the Aztecs. His countenance was distorted, hideous, and emblematic of fierce passion. His right hand wielded a huge bow, and his left held a golden arrow, while his trappings were those supposed by the superstitious people to belong to the deity; yet, the most prominent ornament was a chain of solid gold and silver hearts, strung alternate, and suspended around his neck, indicating the sacrifice in which he took the most delight There was, however, a more evident token of his character in the forms of three human hearts, then smoking and quivering on a golden platter before the huge image. The sight caused a cold shudder to pass over the Spaniards, for alas! they knew not but a similar fate was in reserve for them!

The other temple was devoted to a milder god. It was called, *Tezcatlipoca*, the one who created the world and watched over it. This image was represented as a young man, and was hewn from black stone, highly polished. This god was decorated, and armed as a warrior. His armor and weapons were all garnished with gold and jewels; yet he—like his neighbor—had a peculiar relish for dainty diet, as the Spaniards discovered before him five bleeding hearts, just torn from the reeking breasts of the sacrificed victims.

The walls and floor of these temples, were besmeared with human blood, and the stench was most offensive; while the priests, with garments stiff with the dried blood, and their faces painted with coarse characters of mystic import, moved hurriedly to and fro, among the Spaniards.

From these foul abodes, Cortez gladly retreated, and descended to the hard paved court below, where he made a careful survey of the buildings in the inclosure.

The principal attraction in this quarter, was the schools for the instruction of youth of both sexes, drawn chiefly from the high and wealthy classes. The girls were taught by priestesses, and the boys by male instructors, while the most blameless deportment was rigidly enforced throughout every department of the institution.

During these wanderings, which were extended through every part of the capital, Cortez was always under the immediate eye of Montezuma, to whom he looked for protection, and, but for whose presence, he would have fared as the sacrificial victim in the hands of the excited and insulted populace.

The Spanish general saw every move of the people. He watched them with the eye of a lynx, and detected many circumstances which led him to believe that an open revolt against their sovereign was contemplated; in which case, his own fate, and that of his army, was not a matter of conjecture or probability, but a certainty Every Spaniard in the capital, would die on the sacrificial stone, to appease the wrath of those gods, whom they had seen on the great *teocalli!*

In this trying emergency, Cortez concocted a scheme which none but the most daring man in the most desperate extremity would have conceived.

The crisis had come! Something must be done, and that speedily. Cortez looked around upon his four hundred Spaniards, and his Tlascalan allies, then without the walls of his immediate quarters; then beheld not less than five hundred thousand Aztecs, who were only held in check, out of respect to Montezuma, whom they had so long honored and obeyed.

In the midst of these exciting scenes, Maxtla Ytzcoatl reached the imperial palace, and was soon followed by the tireless Meztli, the half-idiot serving-maid of the caves.

CHAPTER XV

CORTEZ AS THE INVADER AND CONQUEROR.

It was no sooner known to Montezuma that the sculptor was in the palace than a courier was dispatched, demanding an immediate interview. Maxtla obeyed the royal mandate, without hesitancy, and, although questioned by the emperor as to where he had been, he purposely avoided giving a direct answer. The substance of the conferance was an eager desire on the part of the monarch to have the monument completed in the shortest possible time, that he might exhibit the wonderful achievement to his friends—the Spaniards.

Maxtla was surprised at the great change in the actions of the people throughout the entire capital, and apparently of the whole nation, during the past ten days. All business had stopped; everybody was talking; the burden of their conversation was: "The strangers!—The strangers!"

Crowds were continually huddled together at the street corners, earnestly discussing the all-absorbing topic. Nobles and lords from the adjoining cities were hurrying hither and thither; while secret confederations were formed in different parts of the capital—their avowed purpose being to condemn the sovereign in his course toward the detested invaders. Vigilant committees were appointed to watch the progress of the Spaniards, and to note the movements of Montezuma. Couriers were sent into the country, in every direction, calling upon the people to gather in and around the capital, to be ready in case of need.

It was a period of painful suspense to Cortez and his faithful followers; yet this matchless man of nerve was as calm and self possessed as if walking the rounds of his own garden in Havana. He had already matured his plans—such plans as only his daring soul would have conceived, and only his heart of iron and nerves of steel would execute. That plan embraced, in its consummation, the seizure of the hospitable monarch. His idea was, to march to the royal palace, and bear Montezuma back to the Spanish quarters by fair means if possible.

by force if necessary, but, at any and at all hazards, to get possession of his person.

Cortez found a shallow pretext for this remarkable movement, in the fact that two Spaniards had just been murdered in a neighboring province, by order of the governor—Quauhpopoca, one of Montezuma's confidential lords.

With a chosen band of his most trusty followers, the Spanish general visited the imperial palace, and after a few common-place remarks with the sovereign, informed him of his suspicions that he was cognizant of the alleged murders. Montezuma was surprised at the accusation, yet managed to conceal his feelings. The General insisted that the monarch should send and arrest the offenders, irrespective of position, and have them brought to the capital for examination. To this Montezuma consented, and dispatched an officer, empowered with a royal signet, which the sovereign took from his wrist. The messenger was authorized to command Quauhpopoca, and all implicated in the murders, to appear forthwith, at the imperial court. He was also empowered to call upon the people to enforce the mandate if he met with opposition.

When the officer had departed, Cortez assured Montezuma that his prompt action convinced him of his innocence in the plot; but, that it was necessary that *their* great sovereign, across the water, should also be convinced. Nothing would conduce so much to the establishing of friendly feelings as to have the emperor occupy the same palace with the Spaniards, until the examination of the governor was concluded and the matter settled.

Montezuma listened to this proposition with perfect amazement, and replied: "When was it ever known that a great prince like myself, voluntarily left his own palace to become a prisoner in the hands of strangers?"

Cortez assured the indignant monarch, that he should not go as a prisoner, but should meet with the most respectful treatment, and should continue to hold intercourse with and exercise power over his people as usual.

"If I should consent to such degradation," the monarch answered; "my subjects would not."

Two hours were devoted in vain efforts to induce the monarch to accompany them, of his own free will, when a high-mettled cavalier, impatient at the delay, cried out—

"Why do you waste words with the barbarian? We have gone too far to recede now. Let us seize him, and if he resists, plunge our swords into his body."

The fierce tones and gestures of the speaker alarmed the monarch, who inquired of Marina* what was meant. She, under Cortez's instruction, told Montezuma, that it was the command of their sovereign, across the water, when the troubled emperor either through physical or supernatural fear, reluctantly consented to the desires of his conquerors.

Had he possessed the spirit of his nephew, Guatemozin, he would have called his nobles around him, and left his heart's blood on the threshold, ere he would have borne with such unparalleled effrontery as the Spaniards had shown, and have been dragged a prisoner from his own palace.

Cortez gave instant order for the royal *palaquin*, and immediately the monarch was being conveyed to the Spanish quarters. Pride now returned to the emperor, and, since he must be, it should appear with his free will,—a still more fortunate event for the success of the daring enterprise. As the retinue marched through the streets, escorted by the Spaniards, a wild tumult gathered thick around them. So threatening was the mob, that the Spaniards trembled for the result; and, had not Montezuma, by command of his evil genius—for such was Cortez—called out for the people to disperse, not one of those bold adventurers would have reached the garrison.

The mob continued to increase rapidly after Montezuma entered the Spanish quarters, and the monarch was compelled to send out his nobles, ordering the populace to disperse and return to their homes.

They obeyed, but with a bad grace; and it was evident to

---

* At the period of Cortez's triumph over the Tabascans, shortly after his arrival on the coast, he was made a present by the Tobasco chief, of twenty female slaves, among whom was Marina—as she was called by the Spaniards. She was born at Painalla in the province of Coatzacualco, on the southeastern border of the Mexican empire. When she was quite young, she was sold into slavery by her own mother, and eventually became attached to the household of the Tobasco chief, in which position she learned their dialect. She was pleased with the Spaniards, and being naturally much gifted in powers of memory, soon learned the Spanish language, sufficient to be of great assistance to the conquerors, during the period of conquest, as interpreter. She officiated· upon all occasions, as the intermedia of conversation.

Cortez that the feeling of resentment was but checked for a brief period, when it would burst forth with greater force. Still the ever-watchful general hoped, by strong and decided movements, to overawe the populace, and bring them under his subjection.

Could the truth have been known, at that period of Cortez's career, it would have shown that he would have gladly retreated from the capital, could he have seen even a possibility of escape. Hemmed in on all sides by unsurmountable obstacles he presented a bold and defiant front, apparently undaunted in his purpose, but in reality unflinching from the very desperation of his fortunes.

He had accomplished one great achievement, and held a powerful hostage for the future security of himself and his little army; yet, he did not pause, but went still further, and humbled the noble, generous Aztec sovereign, down into the very dust.

When Quauhpopoca, the guilty governor arrived, he was coolly received by his emperor, and referred to Cortez for examination—could he have done otherwise?

Here the Aztec noble was dealt with in a summary manner by the Spaniards, who intended to make a severe example of him, for the special benefit of the natives, hoping thereby to impress them with the might and importance of the power of the invaders.

The governor and his accomplices were sentenced to be burnt alive, and the fagots were drawn by the emperor's permission, from the royal arsenals around the *teocallis*. The piles were immense, and consisted of bows, arrows, javelins, shields, and other weapons—a plan purposely arranged by Cortez, who hoped to destroy as large an amount of the native arms as possible. During this movement the populace looked on with a stupefied astonishment supposing the great sacrifice of property, to be made by command of their sovereign.

The crowning act of Cortez, on this occasion, was a fair characteristic of the man. While the preparations for the execution were going on, the general, attended by one soldier, bearing fetters in his hand, entered the apartment where Montezuma sat brooding over his misfortunes, and, with a severe aspect charged the monarch with having instigated the murders of which his subjects were about to suffer. He then ordered the soldier to place the shackles upon the emperor's ankles, and coolly waited until it was done, then turned short upon his heel, and left the room.

This act rendered Montezuma speechless. He appeared as one struck dumb, and offered no resistance. His faithful attendants, bathed in tears, offered their condolence. They even held his feet in their laps, and inserted portions of their garments between the royal ankles and the cold iron, but they could not reach the iron that had entered the monarch's heart.

Meanwhile, the execution went on, and the victims died with Indian fortitude. Not one muscle moved during the awful ordeal. When the fearful sentence had been executed, Cortez re-entered Montezuma's presence, and, kneeling down, removed the fetters, apologizing for the necessity of subjecting him to such punishment; while the sovereign, whose frown but a week before, would have made the whole nation tremble, was now craven enough to thank his deliverer for his freedom! Such was the effect of the astounding bravado of Cortez.

The nature of our narrative forbids us to enter into a detailed recital of the incidents of that momentous time. The record of facts all reads like a romance which would shame the efforts of any fictionist in contrast. We will, however, gratify the reader, whose attention must be greatly excited in these incidents, by quoting from our late lamented PRESCOTT, to whose elaborate and classic works on the CONQUEST, we are indebted for many of the incidents presented in these pages. He says:

"These events were certainly some of the most extraordinary on the pages of history. That a small body of men, like the Spaniards, should have entered the palace of a mighty prince, have seized his person in the midst of his vassals, have borne him off a captive to their quarters—that they should have put to an ignominious death before his face his high officer, for executing, probably, his own commands, and have crowned the whole by putting the monarch in irons like a common malefactor—that this should have been done, not to a drivelling dotard in the decay of his fortunes, but to a proud monarch in the plenitude of his power, in the very heart of his capital, surrounded by thousands and tens of thousands, who trembled at his nod, and would have poured out their blood like water in his defense,—that all this should have been done by a mere handful of adventurers, is a thing too extravagant, altogether too improbable, for the pages of romance! It is, nevertheless, true!"

Agreeably to the prophecy of Cortez, rigor of action and bravery won the day. Whatever may have been the feeling among the populace they did not exhibit it publicly, but gradually submitted step by step, until the Spanish general had triumphed over the innumerable host of his enemies. He set his foot on the neck of princes, and the great Aztec emperor was but a tool in his hands for accomplishing this work. He then explored the surrounding country, sought out the gold and silver mines, and dove far down into the earth, after precious stones.

While men, under guidance of natives, were performing this work, Cortez caused Montezuma to send out his collectors, that they might visit all the principal cities and provinces, attended by a consort of Spaniards, to receive the customary tribute in the name of the Castilian Crown. To the amount thus collected, Montezuma added an immense treasure on his own account; and when all had been gathered into the Spanish quarters, it formed " three great heaps."

Magnificent as it was, the Aztec monarch regretted that it was no larger, and remarked: " Take it, Malinche"—the name by which he always called Cortez, "and let it be recorded in your annals, that Montezuma sent this present to your master."

Thus passed the first six months of Cortez in the capital, during which time he had lorded it over the country with full sway. At this period, however, a sudden change came over the aspect of his affairs, and every precaution that prudence and good judgment could devise was exercised to meet the threatened emergency. The soldiers ate, drank, and slept, fully armed and equipped, and their horses were ready caparisoned, day and night. The guards were doubled, and the little garrison was nearly in a state of siege.

This untoward movement was occasioned by the Spaniards

interfering with the Aztec religion, thereby incurring the displeasure of the priesthood—the most dangerous point upon which they could have touched.

In all semi-civilized states of society, the priests, as a usual thing, hold unbounded authority. It was thus with the Buddhists of the East—the Brahmins of India—the Magi of Persia—the Druids of early Britain—the priests of Ancient Egypt and Assyria, and those of Mexico.

To add still more to the hazardous position of the Spaniards, on this perilous occasion, tidings reached them from the coast, that a large armed force from Cuba had landed, headed by Panfilo de Narvaez, whose avowed purpose was to capture Cortez as a traitor, and take him in irons to Spain.*

Cortez was sorely puzzled how to proceed under these difficulties; but, as ever, there was a magic influence in his movements, and in a short space of time, he had subdued the threatened Aztec insurrection, placing himself again on good footing, not only with the populace, but with the priesthood, whose wrath he had enkindled by the desecration of their temples and the destruction of their wooden and jewel bedizened deities before whose altars human blood had run like a river. He then turned his attention toward the movements of Narvaez, who having landed and possessed himself of Vera Cruz and the forts near by, was making bold and defiant threats of what he could and would do with the unauthorized invaders. Cortez knew if he remained in the capital where he then was, he could not hope to contend successfully with the formidable force which his rival brought against him, augmented as it would be by the disaffected Aztecs, who would willingly join with him in rescuing their sovereign from the

---

* General Narvaez, was sent to the coast, under the direction, and by authority of Velasquez, governor of Cuba, who was Cortez's most bitter enemy; inasmuch as Cortez had originally sailed from Cuba under the auspices of the same governor. Previous to the sailing of the expedition of Cortez, he saw fit to disregard the injunctions of his patron and superior, and took his own course, irrespective of the governor's orders. Narvaez was a willing tool in the hands of the zealous Velasquez, yet he was deficient in that prudence, foresight, and judgment, which would enable him to cope successfully with Cortez. His squadron consisted of eighteen vessels, and nine hundred men, fully armed and equipped, to take Cortez and his men prisoners at all hazards, and return with them to Cuba for punishment by the crown officers.

grasp of the usurpers. And yet if he marched against Narvaez, he must abandon all he had accomplished, by leaving the capital again in the hands of the emperor.

He finally decided to intrust the garrison, in the capital, to his warm personal friend, Pedro de Alvarado, whom he cautioned to exercise moderation and forbearance, and by all means to keep possession of the Aztec sovereign, for in that rested all their authority in the land.

From Montezuma, Cortez exacted a promise to remain friendly with his people until he returned, assuring him that, if he did, their great sovereign across the water should know it, but, if he proved false, he should be the first to fall. The general then took his leave of the capital, and was escorted across the causeway by Montezuma and a few of his nobles, under a strong guard of Spaniards.

Cortez left one hundred and fifty men in the garrison, with all the artillery, and nearly all the horses; and took with himself only seventy soldiers, with whom to cope with an army of nine hundred veterans, fully armed and equipped, and led by old, experienced generals. The cool, calculating Castilian, did not rely upon strength to accomplish the victory. It must be done with artifice and superior generalship. With this view he marched boldly and confidently into the enemies' country. During this time, he was re-enforced by his own countrymen, previously stationed through the country, and by deserters from Narvaez's army, until his little band numbered two hundred and sixty-six, yet their arms were woefully deficient.

Narvaez was then stationed in the city of Cempoalla, on the eastern coast, and for a time negotiations were carried on between him and his intended victim, yet without resulting in any thing like harmony between the two generals. When all fair means had been exhausted, and Narvaez still decided to pursue his rigid course, Cortez began arranging for a surprise assault.

This bold scheme was carried into effect during an awful storm, which raged with great fury. Cortez and his followers had previously advanced as near to their enemies as was practicable, and, as the night presented the appearance of affording that shelter which they desired, they commenced a stealthy, though hurried march toward the contemplated scene of struggle. They pressed forward without beat of drum or sound of trumpet, while each man fully realized the importance of the movement, and was resolved to die, or conquer.

Entering the suburbs of the city, Cortez was surprised at not finding a thorough system of sentry, and the fact of this deficiency of judgment in so important a point, gave him new courage in the undertaking. The storm raged with unabated fury—the falling torrent, the constant roll of thunder, and the moaning of wind as it swept through the city, deadened the sound of the soldiers' footsteps, enabling them to advance unnoticed.

They could not, however, move stealthily enough altogether to elude notice. Soon the alarm was given. Then followed an exciting scene of bustle and confusion. Dragoons sprang to their feet, artillerymen to their guns; while Narvaez, awakened from a quiet sleep, hurried on his armor and rushed into the fray.

That instant a bright flash lit up a long line of battlement, followed by a deafening sound of cannon, as the artillery poured a mass of shot and canister through the street; but Cortez had previously divided his little company, and each party marched close to the buildings on either side of the thoroughfare. Thus the shot did no execution whatever, and only served to arouse the inhabitants of the little city.

Cortez had now reached the inclosure, surrounding the *teocalli*, where Narvaez and his army were stationed, and without giving them time to reload, he sprang upon the wall, shouting the watchword of the night—

"Espiritu Santo! Espiritu Santo!"

CHAPTER XVI.

IN PRISON AGAIN.

We have anticipated the progress of our story by several months, in order to render consecutive the narrative of Cortez and his drama—shall we say his tragedy? Let us now return to pick up the threads of the story we are weaving, and hasten it to its final consummation.

We saw Mazina restored to Tonatiuh, in her cave-home at the *teocallis*, through the kind offices of the priest, who ever seemed near her when danger threatened, or when his coming could do good. His wonderful ubiquity of bodily presence seemed something preternatural—no space, nor time, nor danger interposed to prevent his unwearied watchfulness over Mazina and Maxtla. Whoever he was—and his impenetrable mask defied all scrutiny of his face—he certainly held the youthful lovers in tender regard, and they seemed to realize something of right and authority in his coming and going. Only in the end can we draw aside that mask to discove whose face and eyes have so long looked behind it.

On the evening after Mazina's return from her imprisonment in the mountain caves, she was seated with Tonatiuh at the entrance of the home of the prophetess. The night was very fair; stars shone overhead like angels' eyes peering through the empyrean of heaven's floor; sweetest airs of orange and palm groves floated around, diffusing that sense of the beautiful which fills the soul with a fullness of peace. So charmed were the hours that they rapidly fled; and far into the night the two still sat at the cave-door, thinking and feeling, rather than to break the silence even by their whispers.

Suddenly they were startled by the cry of an infant, apparently but a short distance away. They listened and heard it again. Both sprang forward in the direction of the sound to discover the child, if child it was, out there in the night, perchance alone. They had not proceeded far, when two men stepped in front of them. Tonatiuh caught Mazina by the arm and sprang back; but it was too late. They were firmly bound together by the wrists, and their faces bandaged, until they could not speak.

"Ah! my pretty one!" sneered Toluca. "Once again I have you in my power, and I give you good security that you do not escape me this time."

One there was whose cunning the villain could not entrap, and she was not absent now to foil and curse her foe:—Metzli saw and heard all; and as Toluca drove his prisoners away, she bounded like a deer on into the city and was soon lost in its shadows and silences.

It was several moments ere the two captives really understood how they were situated, or what had taken place. So sudden and unexpected was the seizure, it was not until Toluca ordered them to proceed that they were fully impressed with the truth of their position, and trembled in view of what they might expect.

It was after midnight when they reached the bank of Tezcuco, near the western causeway, leading to the capital. Here they were ordered into a boat, which lay moored to the beach, and were rapidly but silently pulled across the lake, and soon found the doors of Lord Ahuitzol's palace opening to receive them.

Here the cord was loosened that held the captives together. Mazina was conducted to a large apartment by a slave, thoroughly instructed in his duty. He removed the ligament from her wrists, the bandage from her eyes, and quickly returned, having closed the door upon the maid, securing it upon the outside. She was again a prisoner.

Meanwhile Tonatiuh was escorted to a distant part of the palace, and placed in a small, damp dungeon. Neither the bandage across her mouth, nor the cords on her wrists were removed, notwithstanding they were tied so tight as to be very painful.

At an early hour on the following morning twelve men had been arrested, and cited to appear before Montezuma. They were accused of conspiring against the emperor's life, and, so stricken were they by the emperor's pale, distressed look, that they soon confessed their guilt, implicating Lord Ahuitzol as the instigator of the plot. It appeared that the monarch had been made acquainted with all the proceedings in a mysterious manner. His decision was quickly and firmly pronounced. He ordered that the twelve men be taken to the great *teocalli*, and there offered as a common sacrifice; and he further commanded that Lord Ahuitzol should be summoned to witness the execution of the decree, while his own share in the plot should be made public by the heralds.

That the reader may have some knowledge of this sacrifice, in which so many thousands of the Aztec race perished yearly, not only in the capital but throughout every province, we will dwell a moment upon this bloody, inhuman rite, held sacred by their religion.

Brantz Mayer, in his history of the Conquest, has given us a condensed, yet full description of this fearful holocaust. He says:

"This sacrifice was performed by a chief priest and six assistants. The principal flamen, habited in a red scapulary fringed with cotton, and crowned with a circlet of green and yellow plumes, assumed, for the occasion, the name of the deity to whom the offering was made. His acolytes, clad in white robes embroidered with black, their hands covered with leathern thongs, their foreheads filleted with parti-colored papers, their bodies dyed perfectly black, prepared the victim for the altar; and, having dressed him in the insignia of the deity to whom he was to be sacrificed, bore him through the town begging alms for the temple. He was then carried to the summit of the *teocalli*, where four priests extended him across the curved surface of an arched stone placed on the sacrificial stone, while another held his head firmly beneath a heavy yoke. The chief priest—the *topiltzin* or sacrificer—then stretched the breast of the victim tightly by bending his body back as far as possible, and, seizing the obsidian knife of sacrifice, cut a deep gash across the region of the captive's heart. The extreme tension of the flesh and muscles at once yielded beneath the blade, and the heart of the victim lay palpitating in the bloody gap. The sacrificer immediately thrust his hand into the wound, and, tearing out the quivering vital, threw it at the feet of the idol,—inserted it with a golden spoon into the mouth,—or, after offering it to the deity, consumed it in fire, and preserved the sacred ashes with the greatest reverence. When this horrid rite was finished in the temple, the victim's body was thrown from the top of the *teocalli*, whence it was borne away and converted into a cannibal feast by the populace, or devoted to feed the beasts in the royal menagerie."

How these people, semi-civilized and cultivated as they certainly were, could have tolerated such a horrid rite, is past comprehension. That Montezuma, who, in all his deportment, exhibited a truly noble, humane, and generous disposition, should have sanctioned the practice, not only of human sacrifice, but making feasts of the victim's flesh, is equally incomprehensible, and a subject of wonder.

After Tonatiuh and Mazina were placed in the different apartments in Lord Ahuitzol's palace, Toluca procured a light and visited the cell where the prophetess was imprisoned. Having removed the bandage from her face, he asked her in a sneering tone:

"Do you remember the scene on the island, where you predicted such fearful events yet to take place during my life?"

"I spoke the truth!" she answered.

"You know too much—altogether too much! This little cell is quite large enough for any person having such extensive information," retorted the villain, with hate and fear written upon his every feature.

"Toluca Ahuitzol will yet learn that Tonatiuh has told him the truth. He will yet tremble as a leaf shaken by the wind— humbled in the very dust, and die a felon's death." Her voice was fearfully clear and calm.

"If I do, you shall not bear witness against me!" he retorted, with fire in his serpent-like eyes.

"There are those who will," she replied. "If you have come here to taunt me, you have remained long enough. If you intend to release me at all do so at once, and save yourself the mortification of having others do it for you. I shall not dally words with *you*."

"Ha! ha! ha!" laughed the villain. "You *talk* well, but I tell you that you will *never leave this cell*. You shall die here, rot here; your dust shall lie here, mingled with that of many others who have perished here before you. When I leave you now, and close the door, it will *never be reopened while you live;* so you may be as calm and reconciled as you choose, or you may storm and rave to your heart's content. You see I am *very* obliging. So now, good-by, good mother priest! Go and lay down and die as soon as you can!" he said, as he passed from the dungeon. The door was closed with a dull, heavy sound.

"*Is* this what I shall have to suffer? *Must* I die thus? Is my life to be closed up forever in this dread place? Mazina—" she started suddenly; the door was opened.

"Tonatiuh!" spoke a low voice. "Tonatiuh! You here?"

"Meztli! is that you?" Her voice was husky, with her unusual emotion.

"Yes! Meztli would save you. Here, take my hand quickly, and I will lead you from this dirty cell."

"They are still tied!" exclaimed Tonatiuh, now greatly agitated.

Meztli caught hold of her arm, dragged her into the passage, and from thence into a small recess, off the passage, where they crouched behind a stone seat. Scarce time had they to compose themselves, when Toluca returned, bearing in his hand a ladle of molten lead, which he poured into the socket containing the spring, thus to remove all chance of opening the stone door, except by picking it to pieces.

Tonatiuh witnessed this with a beating heart. It may be guessed that she felt relieved when he again left the passage.

Half an hour later, Tonatiuh had departed from the hated palace, and was crossing the great causeway, leading west from the capital.

Mazina, on being bolted into the apartment by the slave, endeavored to compose her mind to something like tranquillity. She was now in the apartment which she once occupied as her own, and where she had enjoyed many happy days. Then she was free to go and come as she chose; but now she was a prisoner. The door had been closed upon her, and she knew full well for what purpose.

The long, weary, and hurried walk which she had been compelled to undergo, and the agony of mind under which she labored, so prostrated her whole system that she lay down on the edge of her bed, and unconsciously fell into a fitful slumber. Her excited imagination pictured frightful events. In the wanderings of her mind she saw her friends dragged from before her eyes, saw them prosecuted nigh unto death, witnessed their tortures, until the cold perspiration stood in great drops upon her forehead. She was at length aroused by the sound of a footstep, and, on looking up, beheld Toluca, who had just come from the dungeon, where he had, as he supposed, permanently sealed and concealed the fate of Tonatiuh. Mazina sprang from the couch, and fled to the farthest corner of the room, and cried:

"Away from me, monster! Away, I say! I hate your presence, and scorn your power. Away—away!"

"My dear Mazina," he replied, with mock respect, "I thought you would be lonesome, so I came to keep you company for an hour, as I leave the city before sunrise."

"Tell me, sir, why you persecute me in this manner? Have I ever committed an error, punishable with such base treatment as you have dealt out to me and my friends?"

"You are decidedly pointed in your remarks, my dear," he rejoined coolly. "You are mistaken, however, in asserting that I am your enemy, as I am directly the other thing—the best friend you have."

"Your actions exhibit your regard in a remarkably bad light," she haughtily replied. "If you have even respect for me, leave the apartment instantly, and never again force yourself upon my notice. Your conduct is more that of a fiend incarnate, than a human being."

"Really, I could not think of going until I had made a more agreeable arrangement with you;" and there was the sarcasm of a devil in his tone. "You know that I have loved you long and devotedly—that I have, in times past, used every reasonable argument to convince you of my sincerity; but kind words and gentle treatment have had no effect. I therefore concluded to use my own means to obtain the coveted end, and I assure you that you *shall* be mine, either lawfully or unlawfully. You can make your own choice."

Mazina did not reply. The truth of her dreadful position came with overwhelming force upon her heart, and, bowing her head she sobbed aloud.

"I shall leave you for awhile," he added, "but, during my absence you will be under the *especial* care and guardianship of Lord Ahuitzol, and will not be allowed to leave this apartment. Still, you shall be treated in every way as becomes your station. When I return you will understand more fully what I have said;" then, with a haughty air, he strode from the room, securing the door on the outside.

———

Just before sundown on the following day, an old, gray-haired woman, with bent form and palsied limbs, was passing through Lord Ahuitzol's park. She leaned upon two sticks for support, and walked with slow, measured tread. Her garments were clean and tidy, but of coarse material. Around her neck was a cord, to which was attached a basket filled with light toys and ornaments, showing that she made her living by peddling these articles among families who had children.

Having approached near to the palace-entrance, she sat down on a bench, leaned her canes against the seat, and commenced arranging the trinkets from the basket into her lap. She had not sat there long, when Lord Ahuitzol came hurriedly from the palace. Discovering her, he paused an instant. He had, apparently, entertained a thought which quickly vanished, and he passed on, taking no further notice of her, or she of him; but, suddenly he halted, turned back, and inquired if the articles were for sale?

She replied in the affirmative, when he purchased several toys, during which time he watched her closely, then said:

"Do you live about here?"

"I come from Tezcuco," she answered, beginning to replace her merchandise in the basket again.

"Do you follow peddling for a living?"

"I have no one to look after me, and must live as well as you nobles;" and she began to adjust the cord about her neck, preparatory to starting.

"Would you remain with me in the palace if I would **pay you well?**" and he eyed her closely as he spoke.

"I am too old to labor, and need some one to do for me, rather than for me to do for somebody else," she said, rather tartly.

"The work is easy," he continued, growing more earnest; "in fact, there is no work to be done."

"If there is no work to be done, there will be no pay;" and she rose to depart.

"I will pay you in advance" he urged.

"How much?"

"One quill of gold dust a week, and you shall have slaves to wait upon you."

"What do you expect me to do?"

"Be a governess to a young lady, who is insane, and who has to be confined in her room."

The woman shook her head and started on, but stopped short, and remarked: "Is she hard to manage?"

"No, perfectly docile, and continues to assert that she is not crazy."

"I will try it a week," she said, and turned slowly toward the palace.

Soon Lord Ahuitzol and the old woman entered the apartment where Mazina sat weeping. The moment that the old noble appeared, Mazina sprang forward, threw herself on her knees before him, and, with pleading accents cried:

"No, no! Do not say that I am crazy. Do not! You know I am not!"

The old conspirator, turning to the old woman who had accompanied him to the room, coolly said:

"This is the person I want you to take care of. You must not allow her to leave the room under any pretext whatever, nor allow one of the slaves to enter the apartment. If you are faithful you shall be liberally rewarded; if false, you will will never leave the palace alive."

Mazina rose quickly, came close to the woman, laid her hand upon her shoulder, and gazed long and steadily upon her face. She then moved away to a seat in the corner, sat down, bowed her face in both hands, and groaned in the most bitter anguish.

"Such things as you need or desire in any way will be furnished you by asking any of the slaves. I shall instruct them to that effect;" and the old heart of stone left the apartment. He passed directly to his favorite place of resort, the eastern corridor, where he commenced pacing to and fro among the clustering vines. His arms were folded, his gaze downcast, and his appearance that of deep, earnest meditation.

When the sun had set—when the evening shades had gathered thick around, and when darkness brooded over the city, Lord Ahuitzol was still promenading the corridor. His mind did not appear more calm than when he first began his walk. Finally he halted short, struck his hand firmly upon his brow, and, in a low, hissing tone, said :

"Yes, yes! It *must* be done! Maxtla must die! He must be removed! Toluca was a confounded fool that he let him escape, when he had all the advantage, and could have done the job without danger of detection. Now, there is a risk—a great risk, yet it must be accomplished. I have set my hand to this business, and there is no turning back. I have got Mazina safe! Now, to get rid of the sculptor; then the way is clear, and there shall be no accomplices this time! For my part I cannot tell how Montezuma learned the plot against his life, nor how he learned who the conspirators were; but, true it is, they were *all* arrested before daylight the next morning after the first meeting. Montezuma ordered that I should be present when they were sacrificed. I do not really understand the movement. There is something that looks dark about it; but these invading strangers have taken all his attention during the past few days, and it is well for me, perhaps, that they have. I will manage to remove Maxtla first, then for my other plans. I know the apartment where he lodges at the imperial palace, and the room can be entered by means of which he knows very little. There is that strange priest; he has been hanging around the palace all day. I wish I knew who he was. It's dangerous meddling with these priests, but I *will* settle this one's account, if I can get a good chance. Toluca and Cruzilli will be here in a day or two, then look out. Yes, yes! look out! My authority can *not* be trampled upon with impunity; and the proud monarch shall feel the full weight of my vengeance. I will be revenged! I will—" he paused suddenly, turned, and beheld the strange priest standing before him!

4

CHAPTER XVII.

ACCUMULATION OF DISASTERS.

The forty-eight hours subsequent to the incidents of our last chapter, were of momentous interest to the Aztecs. During that period, their sovereign had unwittingly left his royal palace for an abode in the Spanish quarters,—become a prisoner, and a tool in the hands of the scheming Cortez, for the future subjugation of the empire. As might be supposed, matters of a domestic nature were more or less neglected. While certain portions of the community were conspiring against the invaders, another party was carrying out the wicked propensities of their unbridled passions; very few were pursuing their usual peaceful avocations. The affairs of government were in a sad condition,—circumstances which rendered Toluca and Cruzilli's schemes the more easily accomplished: they could now return to the city and prosecute their base designs without fear of being molested.

It was the hour of midnight, when a man closely muffled about the face, entered the imperial court-yard, and moved hurriedly along through the dense crowd collected around the royal palace, clamorous with indignation and excitement.

Guatemozin had been addressing them on the subject of their sovereign's unexpected step, his sentiments had been expressed in bold, open language; yet, by his command, the enraged populace immediately dispersed, though not until they had pledged themselves, to a man, to stand by the prince in freeing their country of the Spaniards.

While these things were transpiring, Mazina, and the old nurse, provided by the noble, were seated in the apartment into which Mazina was taken by Toluca's orders. The few days in which they had been together, Mazina had completely exhausted herself in trying to engage her indifferent companion in conversation; but was barely able to obtain replies to her questions.

They sat in perfect silence. A deep melancholy rested upon the features of Mazina, while there was a marked sadness brooding over the countenance of her strange companion. During the few days of their acquaintance, Mazina had often detected the woman's attention placed upon her, and frequently noticed that she eyed her with a fixed gaze.

"You do not think that I am crazy, do you?" inquired Mazina, suddenly arousing herself.

"How can I tell?" was the answer. The old woman arose and left the room, leaving Mazina amazed at her conduct.

The woman had not been gone many minutes, when the door was reopened carefully, and a form glided into the room. Mazina did not look up, supposing, of course, that it was her who left the room a moment before, as no other person except Lord Ahuitzol and Toluca had entered the apartment, since she was imprisoned in it.

"Mazina!" She started up with a bound.

"Maxtla!"

In an instant they were clasped in each other's arms.

"Maxtla!" she cried: "How did you reach this, my prison house, which is guarded day and night?"

"Friends are near you, dear Mazina, and I have come to bid you be of good cheer. Our wrongs shall be carried to the emperor, where they will be redressed, and our enemies punished."

"I was just thinking," she remarked, "and wondering if we should ever again be happy as we used to. I was thinking—" she paused, her eyes filled with tears, her heart swelled, and she nestled close to his side. Arousing herself with a great effort, she added: "They say that I am crazy. Lord Ahuitzol makes this cruel accusation, and does not allow me to leave this room, nor to see any person except the old nurse whom he has engaged to wait upon me. Do you think I am insane?"

"No, dear Mazina! but let them consider you so. Perhaps it will be best for the present, that you do not oppose them in this. A few days more, and this matter will be settled, when we shall be married and be beyond the reach of our enemies."

"Oh, that we may! 'Tis awful to be thus persecuted." Then seeming suddenly to recollect more forcibly how they were situated, she added: "We must not remain here a moment. Let us fly instantly. If Lord Ahuitzol should happen to find you here, I fear he would do you harm, in his anger."

"Have no fear of that, for he is a coward alone. All his villainy consists in plotting against defenseless women, who can not easily escape his machinations, and in concocting schemes for more daring ones to execute."

During this colloquy, the door had been left a little ajar, and a pair of bright, keen eyes were peering through the aperture, upon the lovers.

The muffled figure, before alluded to, after stealthily reconnoitering, entered the apartments assigned by Montezuma to the sculptor. All was silent there, was Maxtla asleep? The spy would see. Moving noiselessly toward the sleeping-rooms, all was suddenly illumined with a brilliancy surpassing the sun's brightest rays. The man sprang backward and fairly staggered under the intensity of the light. In a moment he looked around: there stood Tonatiuh, the prophetess, directly before him, eyeing him with flashing orbs.

"Let Toluca Ahuitzol tremble, for Tonatiuh has spoken! He can not escape the fate to which his deeds have brought him."

Toluca stood as one struck dumb. His muffling had fallen from his head and face, and his eyes glared wildly upon the figure before him. There was something so mystical and strange in her appearing to him as she did, that it filled his mind with superstitious fear, and, with frantic haste he fled from the room. His steps echoed to a wild taunting laugh.

The room was immediately enshrouded in darkness again, and the woman of magic passed out into the open court.

Toluca, thus foiled in his attempt to assassinate his rival, hurried away from the scene. Reaching the outside of the wall, surrounding the royal palace, he found Cruzilli awaiting his return, and they passed away together.

The same time that Toluca left the royal palace, Maxtla took his leave of Mazina, counseling her to be of good cheer, and remain where she was until the matter was permanently arranged by the emperor. He went forth from the presence of her he loved, with more hope than he had experienced for many days, and he wandered on through the great park, elated with the prospect. He had proceeded but a short distance, when two men sprang out upon him, with such impetuosity, that, before he could resist, he was felled to the ground, bound hand and foot, drawn to a boat near by, and thrown into it, followed by Cruzilli, who rowed off toward the great channel that led into the lake of Tezcuco.

On the following morning, Mazina arose refreshed. It was considerably after midnight when she retired, but such a load had been removed from her heart, that the few hours of undisturbed repose had quieted her nerves, and restored much of her former buoyancy of spirit.

"Only a few days, he said, when they should be wedded, and forever be happy!" This thought possessed her whole being: she seemed to know no prison bars, but to walk on air. Her old attendant she welcomed with a smile, and she was about to make some playful remark, when a low rap was given on the door, and Toluca entered. A chill passed over Mazina's heart, and her spirits sank with sudden heaviness into their old depths of sorrow. It was the first time his detested form had darkened the door since the night she was placed in the room as a prisoner, and she readily conjectured that his presence at this time boded no good. She hoped that Maxtla would have seen the emperor, and arranged for their wedding, ere Toluca returned from the mountains; but, in this, she was disappointed.

"Ah! fair lady, I am glad to return once more, that I may commune with you, and I hope that we never again shall be separated for any great length of time."

He waited a moment for her answer, then added:

"I trust you have decided to look upon my suit with more favor."

"I have not changed my mind, since I last spoke with you upon this subject," she replied. "The decision which I then made, is still the same."

The old attendant left the apartment, but remained outside listening with great earnestness.

"It matters not what your decision *was*," he continued, with a slight show of anger. "It will avail you little, if 'tis *now* in opposition to my desires. You must be my wife!"

"Not while living;" was the determined reply.

"Then when dead!" was the cool response. "Living or dead, you shall be mine."

"Never, you hated wretch!"

"Spare your invectives, my lady, and be a submissive wife," he remarked, throwing unusual disdain into his tone. "I came only to inform you that we shall be privately married in this room, at sundown this evening, when you will accompany me from the capital, to my home in the mountains."

She grew faint at the words, and could hardly utter:

"I am crazy, Lord Ahuitzol says. You do not wish to wed one who is mad?"

"You have heard my decision. So sure as we both live till evening, so sure shall we be married." Without giving her time to make a reply, he turned and left the room, meeting, as by accident, the attendant at the door. He was soon out of sight in the distant rooms of the palace.

Mazina had maintained her firmness during this scene, with remarkable fortitude, but the door no sooner closed, than she wept convulsively.

"O, Maxtla! Maxtla!" she sobbed. "Why did I not fly with you? Why did you counsel me to remain in the power of these soulless villains? You said that I had friends near. Where are they? Now, if ever, do I need a friend. I will elude the vigilance of my keepers, and seek the emperor. He shall—" She was interrupted by the old attendant, who came hurriedly into the apartment, bearing a bundle of clothes upon her arm. Her movements and appearance were so changed, that Mazina was speechless with wonder.

The woman handed her the clothes, and said:

"Exchange your garments for these. Do it in the shortest possible time."

Mazina did not move.

"As you value your own life and happiness," the woman continued, "obey me, *immediately!*"

Mazina did obey. Assisted by the woman, her robes were soon exchanged for others, and the twain passed rapidly from the room, and through the thick foliage of the park, toward the canal.

They were soon seated in a light canoe, gliding swiftly over the waters of Tezcuco, in a westerly direction. As they reached the beach, the strange priest was observed coming toward them. Mazina rushed eagerly forward, begging his protection, and urged to be conducted to Tonatiuh, if she too had escaped from Toluca.

The priest bade her be of good heart, as friends were near. For a few moments, Mazina appeared lost in thought, but soon recovering, she looked smilingly around—there, in the place of her old attendant, stood Tonatiuh herself. One instant, and they were clasped in each others arms.

It required considerable argument to convince Mazina that her old, palsied, unsociable companion at the palace, was Tonatiuh; but, after having been shown the outer garments, which the prophetess had worn over her own gay robe, the white hair which had concealed her bright glossy tresses, and the potent vial from which she had stained her complexion; the astonished Mazina was forced to believe.

Tonatiuh and Mazina soon sought the secret chambers, while the priest returned in the canoe to the capital.

Cruzilli, with Maxtla, bound and gagged, glided along the channel, until the boat was out upon the smooth, broad bosom of the lake, when he bent to the oars with a will, and the light bark shot as an arrow over the waters.

It was near daylight when he reached the northern beach, about one mile west of Tepejacac. Here he placed stronger ligaments on the prisoner's wrists, and untied those around his ankles. He then ordered him to step out on the land.

There was no alternative but to obey, and trust to fortune to escape, or obtain the advantage. Cruzilli sprang from the boat, struck the captive a heavy blow, and bade him proceed as he should direct, assuring him that the least obstinacy, or appearance of opposition, would be punished with instant death.

In this manner they hurried onward, and it was sundown ere they began to descend the mountains toward the north, during which time, Maxtla had not tasted food or drink, and had suffered great agony from the cruel manner in which he was bound.

But he was destined still to endure. All that night he was compelled to travel at a rapid pace, and his strength was fast failing. He had tried his utmost to sever the cords on his wrists, or remove the gag from his mouth, but in vain. His inhuman captor laughed at his pain, and mocked his sufferings. Every groan was rewarded with a blow, every falter with a curse and a goad, until his trail was marked plainly by his blood.

As the first gray light of morning lit up the eastern horizon, they came upon the camp of a wandering tribe, with whom Cruzilli seemed familiar, and to whom he sold his captive as a slave, a greater punishment to the Aztec than death itself.

CHAPTER XVIII.

FROM THE CAGES TO THE FIELD OF CARNAGE.

The nature of our narrative forbids that we should detail the incidents which marked the career of Cortez in his conquest of Mexico. The whole record would, as we have already written, read like an Arabian Nights tale—so full of the wildest romance is the entire history of that conquest. We have introduced the conqueror and his achievements so far as they had rela'' on to our more individual story; and we shall now pass over as briefly as possible that most wonderful period of time when the Spaniards accomplished the subjugation of the Aztecs.

We left Cortez on the battlements, at Cempoalla, with the cry upon his lips of *Espiritu Santo!* as he rushed upon Narvaez. That cry was the precursor of victory. The emissary of Velasquez was not only conquered, but his well-equipped army became the compatriots of Cortez in the conquest. With recruited fortunes and forces, he again turned his face westward, for the most alarming accounts had come from the little garrison left in the capital:—the natives were all up in arms determined upon the extermination of the Spaniards. The cruel Alvarado had murdered, in cold blood, *six hundred* of the flower of the Aztec nobility, as they were gathered at one of their annual feasts, and this act had stirred up in the hearts of the people a fire of hate, which only the blood of the invaders could extinguish. Cortez arrived after forced marches at the capital, to find all in a state of siege. Business was entirely suspended—the whole country around swarmed with Indians ready for the charge. That charge came. It seemed as if the very stones of the earth became Indians—their numbers were so many. They swarmed every avenue of approach to the Spanish quarters, and though the cannon and musket balls mowed them down like grain, ten seemed to arise out of the bloody corpse of one. Against such odds no force could stand, and Cortez planned a retreat—the most memorable that burdens the page of human history with its story of human prowess and courage. The captive emperor, Montezuma, was, as a last hope prior to the retreat, brought to the battlements by order of Cortez, to exert his authority to compel his people to cease hostilities, as the Spaniards had all promised to leave the country. That act was his last. His countrymen, maddened by his weakness and submission in such an hour, pierced him with arrows and he was borne away to die—an omen of the fortunes which awaited his people after the very waters of the lake were crimsoned with their life-blood. In the midst of these scenes Lord Ahuitzol moved—a very spirit of the fight. His hate of his sovereign impelled him to violence; and when Montezuma appeared upon the battlements, to reason with his people, it was Cruzilli's arrow, sped by the old lord's order, which gave the monarch his death wound. But there was vengeance in store for those two men of blood. An Aztec, of slender, lithe form sprung up the battlements—made a sign of the cross to the Spaniards—seized a musket, and sent a ball with unerring aim into the old lord's heart. Cruzilli was not spared—that priest of the mask saw his act of murder, sprang to his side and with wonderful celerity toppled the brute over the *azotea* walls to the ground.

With this prelude to the events of this chapter, let us resume the narrative.

Tonatiuh and Mazina, made good their escape to the secret chambers after having parted with the priest on the western beach of the lake, after their escape and flight from Lord Ahuitzol's palace.

Here they lived in comparative peace for seven months, and up to the time when Cortez returned from his expedition against General Narvaez on the coast, to encounter perils in the capital, which might well appal even his bold heart.

During this interval, Mazina had not ventured even into the outer cave; while Tonatiuh, having assumed the disguise of a basket-maker, occupied the little cavern. In this position she had often detected Toluca, lurking around, watching the premises; yet he failed to recognize, in the coarse habited basket-maker, either Tonatiuh, the prophetess, or the old palsied attendant at the palace.

The friendly priest had not visited the secret chambers during this entire time, though Tonatiuh had often seen him in the capital, to which place she went to dispose of her merchandise. Let us now look in upon Mazina, as she sat there in her comfortable prison, and see how the lapse of time has affected her.

She was pale, her cheeks were wasted, her eyes sunken, while there was an unnatural uneasiness in her movements. Her long tresses hung loose around her shoulders; her robe was neat, but no ornaments were upon her person, except a gold locket and chain on her neck. She had been seated one day, in a long reverie, from which, with apparent effort, she aroused herself, while these words dropped slowly from her lips:—

"Oh, this suspense is dreadful! Seven long months since I have heard a word from Maxtla, and he cannot be found in the whole capital. I fear—I *know* evil has befallen him. Tonatiuh says the priest has made use of every effort in his power to learn where the sculptor is. I think he has been killed. 'Tis fearful to contemplate, but I am sure that he has been murdered, else he would have sought for me here. This would not have occurred but for the Spaniards in the capital. Montezuma was once my warm friend, and I believe he is now, but he is a prisoner and has little time to attend to petty domestic affairs. O Maxtla! where are you? Why do you not"—

She was interrupted by Tonatiuh, who, having just returned from the capital, came suddenly into the apartment, and exclaimed: "Mazina! there are fearful times in the city. A very large army of Spaniards entered it yesterday, and the people are preparing to attack them in their garrison. It will be an awful moment, and I should not wonder if half the capital were destroyed."

"And what of Maxtla?" Mazina inquired.

"Not a word of him or Meztli; you remember she disappeared about the same time. I saw the priest, but I could not obtain an opportunity to speak with him. He appeared terribly excited and all engaged with the stirring events. He is a strange man. I wish I *could* see his face."

It will be remembered that Maxtla was sold into slavery by

Cruzilli without being allowed to partake of food or water, he was roughly blindfolded, and hurried forward between two stalwart men. They traveled many leagues in this manner, when his conductors halted, and held a short consultation. A peculiar sound, as of a bird chirping was heard, when one of the men caught hold of his prisoner's arm, and dragged him down a flight of stone steps into a narrow, damp passage. Still they hurried forward over a rough course, until they had, apparently, reached a distance of several hundred feet into the very bowels of the earth. Presently they came to another halt, when the bandage was removed from his eyes, the gag from his mouth, and, from exhaustion, he fell helpless on the stone floor. One moment and he was alone in a dark cell, with a heavy door closed upon him.

His face and wrists were swollen and very painful, and his system greatly reduced from loss of proper nourishment; still, he managed to rise to his feet, and moved around in the dark cave to learn if possible the situation and condition of his present quarters. Ere long a door opened and a flood of light from a flaming torch, lit up the cell. For an instant, the sudden change rendered him almost blind, but he soon became accustomed to the brilliancy, and gazed with anxious interest upon the person who held the torch. It was a large, muscular man, dressed in the hieroglyphic garb of a priest, with a savage expression of features. In one hand he held the torch, in the other, a heavy *maquahuitl*. After having watched his victim for a few moments, he said:

"We have purchased you at a great price of your captor, to offer as a sacrifice to the war-god, *Huitzilopotchli*, who is angry at the sacrilege of the profane strangers in the capital. The god is wrath with them, and he must be appeased, or the nation will be destroyed."

It may be supposed that Maxtla trembled, knowing, as he did, the laws of his country in these matters. There was no redress, not even by the interposition of the emperor himself, if the priesthood had marked the victim.

"You will remain here," remarked the priest, without appearing to notice the effect of his words; "until the hour assigned for the sacrifice, during which time your bodily wants shall be well cared for."

The priest then laid down his sword, approached the sculptor, and unbound his arms. That instant, Maxtla sprang to his feet, bounded upon the priest, with the fierceness of a tiger, and hurled him to the hard stone floor. His strength, however, was not sufficient to the task, and, in a few moments he was rebound, this time hand and foot, and left prostrate on the floor.

This over-exertion, caused Maxtla to swoon, in which condition he lay, he knew not how long. When he awoke, the cell was again illumined with the rays of a torch, and, turning his head so that he could discover who carried the light, he beheld an old woman. There was that in her features, which for an instant engaged his attention. He gazed steadily upon her. She started back, held the torch above her head, and returned his gaze. Then approaching, looked steadily in his face, and exclaimed :

"Maxtla Ytzcoatl ! How came you here ?"

That voice—that face ! Surely they were those of his long absent godmother—she who had nurtured him in youth, and had loved him tenderly always. He had not seen her since his residence in the capital. It was joy, indeed, to meet her now when his soul was tortured and his body suffered so in pain.

"Mother Ytzcoatl," he replied : "Hard and cruel fortune brought me here ; but why are you here ? and where are we ?"

"We are beneath a temple," she answered. "I was ordered to prepare you for the sacrifice, but I fear the victim will have flown ere the priests are ready. What say you, my son, would you rather return to the capital ?"

"Ay, good mother ! indeed I would. I have no relish for this manner of appeasing the wrath of the indignant god. Do untie these cords, for they pain me dreadfully."

The woman removed the ligaments, and bathed his wrists, while he related to her the circumstances of his capture and what he had suffered.

She immediately provided him with food and drink, and in a week he was wholly recovered. During this time, he had not seen any person except Mother Ytzcoatl, who had charge of the *teocalli*, kept the sanctuary clean, and waited upon the victims designed for sacrifice.

There were at least fifty cells beneath this temple, which could be entered through a long, intricate passage from the side of a mountain, or from the *teocalli* itself. These cells were devoted exclusively to the use of persons intended for sacrifice. It was customary for the priest to buy slaves of wandering tribes, or elsewhere, as circumstances might offer. The unfortunate victims were then taken to these cells, where they sometimes were kept for years before being offered to the idols. During this time, they enjoyed all the luxuries of life, except their freedom. When once they were placed in these stalls—so to speak—they never left them until taken to the sacrificial block, there to be butchered like dumb brutes.

Maxtla did not remain in the cell, during the week that he had been in the locality, but was with his old nurse and friend, Mother Ytzcoatl. They had much to relate. As soon, however, as practicable, he was anxious to return, for he knew that Mazina would be uneasy at his long absence.

When every thing was prepared for him to make a successful escape, his deliverer requested him to accompany her as she furnished the captives with food. He consented readily, for he had a curiosity to see the variety of subjects for sacrifice. Having provided themselves with a torch, they left Mother Ytzcoatl's private apartments, and entered a long, wide hall, with a row of small cells or "cages," on either side. These cells had a heavy outside door, and a strong inside grate. The former was generally open, while the latter was never moved, except when the victim was being placed in, or taken out.

There were fifty of these cages—twenty-five on a side, and nearly every one held a prisoner. Some were playing, some singing, and some sleeping; while others were weeping, moaning, and exhibiting the most heart-rending grief, in view of the fate to which they had been doomed; yet, so perfectly accustomed to these scenes had the old attendant become, that she was indifferent alike to rejoicing or sorrow.

These cells were, many of them, well furnished with articles of comfort, and ventilated by means of large pipes that extended to the *teocalli* above. The last one they visited was somewhat different from the others, inasmuch as it had no grated door. They passed into this apartment, and beheld a woman crouched in one corner. Her head was bowed in her lap, and she did not take any notice of them.

When Maxtla spoke in answer to some remark of his companion, the captive started, looked up, and, in a moment sprang forward, crying:

"O Maxtla! Save me! Save me! In remembrance of the good deed I once did for you and yours, while in the caves, save me from this fearful—this awful fate!"

"Meztli!" stammered the astonished young man. "Can it be possible that you are here?"

"Yes! yes! I am here!" she sobbed, wringing her hands and weeping aloud. "Oh, save me! Lord Ahuitzol captured me, and sold me to the priests for a sacrifice. If you will save me, I will be your slave—serve you faithfully as long as I live."

As might have been expected, Maxtla was not long in determining what course to pursue in reference to the unfortunate captive, and through his intercession she was set at liberty, and prepared to accompany him to the capital. In an hour they were out upon the open field, pushing on toward the city with all possible dispatch, and nothing occurred to impede their progress, until they had reached within a short distance of Tepejaca, at the terminus of the northern causeway, leading to the capital.

Here they were overtaken by pursuers, who had followed them, and were thrown into prison to await orders from the *teocalli* from which they had escaped.

In this situation they lay until the day previous to the wounding of Montezuma, at which time all the prisons in the nation were thrown wide open, and the inmates forced to join in the attempt to drive the Spaniards from the country.

It had been a long, tedious period to Maxtla and Meztli, for they were kept in close confinement, and not allowed to hold any conversation with persons outside the prison; but, when the doors were opened, by order of Cuitlahua, Montezuma's brother, Maxtla made all haste to the capital. Everywhere he beheld the devastation of war, and the wildest state of excitement prevailed among all classes. With a frenzy almost to insanity, he wandered hither and thither, in search of Mazina, or some one who could give him intelligence of her present situation. There had been such change in the capital that his heart failed him, when he thought that she might be dead—perhaps in the power of Toluca, or under the persecution of her guardian, Lord Ahuitzol. The thought set his brain in a frenzy of excitement, and he hurried about from one locality to another, rushing madly through the dense crowd that thronged the thoroughfares.

He approached the Spanish garrison, and in a moment, discovered Lord Ahuitzol standing upon a high eminence, almost above the fortress. The sight of the plotting villain brought words of imprecation to Maztla's lips, and, involuntarily, his grasp tightened upon the hilt of his *maquahuitl*. Then he heard the sharp report of a musket, and saw the old noble pitch headlong down upon the hard stone pavement. While still contemplating the event, his ears were saluted with a wild laugh, and on looking up again, he beheld Mextli, with her flowing robe, long waving hair, and a short lance in her hand, standing upon the very summit from which the old noble had fallen.

Maxtla eagerly watched the movements of Meztli. Soon a heavy hand was laid upon his shoulder. Turning, he beheld the strange priest, standing directly in front of him.

"Mazina!" exclaimed Maxtla. "Where is she?"

"Safe!" was the reply. "Have no fear of her. She is beyond the reach of her persecutors."

"Dead?" quickly interposed Maxtla.

"No! she is alive and well; but more of this hereafter. You must now aid the Spaniards to subdue the city."

Maxtla was confounded.

"Why aid the Spaniards?" he repeated.

"Because," answered the priest, "in their triumph is your peace; their defeat is for you a prison and the sacrificial knife."

In as few words as possible, Maxtla, in answer to the priest's inquiries, related all that had occurred to him since the time he was seized by Cruzilli in Lord Ahuitzol's park.

While they were talking, the battle raged with great fury. There was a continual roar of cannon, a sharp crackling of musketry, and the fierce yells of the Aztecs, as they rushed madly to the assault.

CHAPTER XIX.

THE HASTENING OF EVENTS, OF STORY AND HISTORY.

On the fourth evening following Montezuma's death, Mazina was walking slowly to and fro in her lonely home. Her mind was troubled with painful forebodings. Maxtla had been gone many—many months, and no tidings came from him. One long week had Tonatiuh been gone. She promised to return in two days. What could have detained her? Was she too, taken from her? Had all her friends been snatched away? What could she do? Where could she fly? Alas! nowhere! She had no place of refuge. Tonatiuh had exacted of her a solemn promise not to leave the chambers under any circumstance, until she returned. Thus far, she had kept her word, but could she always? She had heard the roar of cannon, and watched the smoke as it settled down upon the city and lake, apparently to conceal the work of death and destruction that was going on; while, at night the conflagration of burning buildings presented a grand, yet awful scene.

That strange locket, with its mysterious portrait, so like herself; and the great interest expressed by Tonatiuh, that it should not be lost, appeared to have a meaning which she did not understand. She had seen Tonatiuh's eyes fill with tears as she examined the locket. She had noticed the prophetess tremble with agitation as she viewed the likeness, and she wondered what it all meant. She had questioned her, urging an explanation, but was always put off, without being satisfied.

Why did the strange, kind-hearted woman exhibit such deep affection for her? Why was she so mindful of her interest? The strange priest, whom she had known from childhood, yet never saw his face; why should *he* manifest such remarkable interest for her and Maxtla? Why did he use his influence to bring them together? Why did he ever encourage their intimacy? and why was he ever near to warn and defend them from danger?

Such were the thoughts which passed through her mind, as she walked slowly forward and back in that lonely chamber, far into the night.

Hark! she heard footsteps ascending the stairs. Her heart bounded wildly; her limbs trembled violently. The curtain was pushed aside, and Tonatiuh came into the room. She bounded forward with an exclamation of joy. Their hearts beat one against the other in a tearful joy.

Tonatiuh brushed the disheveled hair back from her companion's brow, and looked down into her young eyes with an expression of intense love, as she said:

"Rejoice my child, for Maxtla lives! I saw him to-day, before the Spanish garrison. He was with the good priest, and I have hurried to bring you the glad news!"

"Thank God!" broke from her lips. "That assurance gives me new life. I now have something to live for; but, will he not come and see me?"

"The priest has doubtless told him where you are, and 'tis probable that he will come as soon as he can. I shall see him to-morrow, if possible."

"Do, dear mother, do. I *must* see him, or my heart will surely break;" and again the tears rolled down her cheeks.

Tonatiuh soon prepared to depart again. She first cautioned her charge to remain quiet, and not leave the chambers until she returned. They then embraced each other with a fervent kiss, and separated.

Mazina listened to the receding footsteps of Tonatiuh, until she heard the outer door close; then gave herself up to her conflicting emotions. It must have been late at night, when she was startled by a sound on the steps, ascending to the chamber, she sprang to her feet. The curtain was again pushed aside, and Maxtla, accompanied by the priest, entered the apartment. One scream, and the suffering girl lay folded to the breast of her lover, in a state of perfect unconsciousness. She was, however, speedily restored, when their reunion was one of bliss too great for expression.

After awhile, their lips found words to relate their wonderful experiences, the strange priest sat a silent listener: and not until the gray tinge of morning was visible in the east, did Maxtla and the priest prepare to depart. Urging Mazina to be cheerful, the two brave men stepped out into the morning twilight, and were soon gone toward the city, where the great battle for life and country and glory was so soon to be fought and won and lost again forevermore.

Another step! A noise in the outer chamber. Now it was in the passage-way. Was one of her friends returning? She had thrilling thoughts of a kiss from Maxtla, as the step drew near, and stood with open arms to welcome her beloved. The curtain opened. She sprang back with an exclamation of alarm, for the detested Toluca stood before her!

"So, so! my pretty bird," he said with a sneer; "you are caught at last."

Toluca came boldly forward, and laid his hand upon her shoulder, when she darted away as from the touch of a leper, and cried:

"Oh, leave me! Why are you here, hated man? Leave me to myself!"

"Indeed!" he replied; "I could not think of it. I have sworn that you should be mine, dead or alive, and I meant what I said. This night I will fulfill my oath, so you may as well be quiet. You are now in my power, beyond interference."

The blood had almost ceased to throb in her veins, and her heart lay still in her breast. Horror stared her boldly in the face. She strove to nerve herself for the unequal struggle.

"I shall not submit to any insult," she firmly said; "I shall defend myself as best I can, from your polluting touch. Wretch, I scorn you!"

"So I suppose," responded the villain, indifferently. "I have had, already, sufficient experience to convince me of that; but, submit you *shall*. These walls are strong and thick; and, if they were not, it would make no difference, as no one is near to hear. I could not have asked, nor planned a more fitting place to compel you to my purposes."

"Toluca!" and Mazina was deathly calm. "So sure as the gods give me life, I will strike you down. Away with you, I say, or by the great sun, I will let out your heart's vile blood!"

"I like your spirit, by the gods!" he remarked, with a hateful smile. "I fancy your courage, indeed I do;" and he stepped forward with extended arms.

"Back! villain!" she cried in agony of spirit. "Back! I say, ponder one moment, ere you move another step."

"Ponder?" he answered, in a mocking tone, while his eye burned with its hellish fire. "Ponder? I did that months ago. Then you scoffed at my professions of love, and laughed at my discomfiture. Now the scales have turned. 'Tis for me to sneer and scoff; but why tarry? Come! I would fold you to my heart," and again he moved forward.

Mazina sprang quickly to one side, drew from her bosom a short blade of *itztli*, and made an attempt to reach the passageway leading from the chambers; but, in an instant, a strong arm was clasped around her waist. She struck with all her strength. The blade entered deep into the right side of the villain, cutting a fearful, yet not fatal wound.

So unexpected was the blow, that he suddenly let go his hold, staggered back a few paces, and exclaimed:

"You have murdered me!"

"I warned you in time, but you would not believe me," she firmly replied. "I will die, before submitting to insult. If you approach me, you do so at your peril. I am desperate—made so by your cruelty."

"We will see!" and again he advanced, but this time more cautiously, but with determination written upon his face.

At that instant, Meztli, a Spanish stiletto in her hand, and eyes fairly flashing fire, came into the chamber.

"Fiend!" she shouted. "Back, or I will sink this weapon in your perjured heart. Back I say!" and her dark eyes glittered like steel as she spoke.

Toluca was thunderstruck. For a moment he appeared undecided what course to pursue, while his gaze was fixed upon her with evident uneasiness.

She stood firm and resolute, her hand grasping tightly the ivory hilt of her keen stiletto.

"Will you leave the room, or shall I force you from it?" he hissed, his voice husky with rage. "I will not be foiled by a woman. Stand back!"

Meztli's foot was moving carefully along on the floor, ap-

parently feeling for some particular point. Toluca stepped
defiantly in front of her, and with a fierce gesture, pointed to
the passage.

Meztli's face was colorless, but as defiant as the inflexible
stone.

"Will you go?" the now foiled and wounded wretch
shouted.

"No!"

"Then I ——"

A quick gasp followed. Toluca disappeared suddenly
through an opening in the floor, caused by the falling of a
trap-door, on which he stood. Down, down he went into a
deep, dark chasm, striking heavily on the bottom.

Meztli did not move; she did not appear to breathe. Mazina
was dumb with amazement, and trembled violently. A low
moan came up from the depths below. Mazina sprang forward,
wound her arms around Meztli's neck, and wept as a child.

"Do not weep, my friend. I have done a deed for which
the gods will not be angered," said the pallid, passionless girl,
"Toluca is a villain, and ought to die. It was he, who murdered my mother—did it in cold blood, in the little cave below, because she befriended *you*. Now, let him lay and consider upon his past deeds. He will have ample time for reflection, and abundance of wickedness to revert to." Saying
this, she waved her hand and was gone.

Mazina was alone over that chasm, from which came a voice
of suffering and despair!

The sun had not advanced far up in the heaven's on that
eventful morning, when Tonatiuh rushed into the secret
chambers where Mazina sat weeping. The old prophetess
was frightful to gaze upon. Her hair was tangled and matted
around her head; her features were covered with wounds and
blood; her eyes were red and inflamed, and glared like the
fires of Popocatepetl.

Mazina sprang to her feet, stared wonderingly upon her
friend, who reeled forward, fell heavily on a stool, and exclaimed:

"Lost! Lost! All is lost!"

Mazina clasped her arms around Tonatiuh's neck, and begged to know the cause of her great grief

"Lost! lost!" sobbed the strange woman, her eyes filling with tears. "All is lost!"

"What is lost?" inquired Mazina, brushing back the damp locks from her friend's brow. "You are badly wounded! Your face is cut terribly; and you are all covered with blood."

"Not dangerously wounded in body, but mortally at heart. I will tell you, so that you can understand. Our peace and future happiness, depend upon the success of the Spaniards over the Aztecs. I know that you think this strange, but, by and by, you will understand it better. Last night, the Spaniards attempted to leave the capital. They were blockaded, and all means of obtaining provisions or water, were cut off by the Aztecs. While Montezuma lived, they had hope of ultimate triumph; but, after his death, Cuitlahua was made emperor. He, possessing a more warlike spirit than his predecessor, soon placed the Spaniards in a dangerous position. Cortez planned his order of retreat, and attempted to carry it into effect last night. The result was one of the most desperate and fearful struggles this nation ever experienced, and the Aztecs were victorious. They destroyed all but a few of the Spaniards, who are now fleeing precipitately—alas! they know not where."

"I heard the tumult," Mazina answered; "but I had so much, and such deep trouble, that I paid little heed to what I heard. Toluca is now in a deep chasm beneath this floor."

Tonatiuh started like one touched with fire.

"What did you say?" she exclaimed.

Mazina related all that had occurred during the past few days—how she had seen Maxtla and the priest,—the unexpected intrusion of Toluca, with a minute recital of the scene that passed between them, and the incomprehensible interposition of Meztli, who foiled the villain by precipitating him through a trap-door in the floor.

Tonatiuh, like Mazina, was surprised to learn that there was such an aperture in the floor.

"I am glad that he is safe!" Tonatiuh said. "Henceforth, we shall, probably, have no more trouble with him. Meztli is a determined and a courageous girl."

"A great-hearted one also," added Mazina; "but, what of

these strangers, of whom you were speaking? Are they not our country's enemies?" and she looked inquiringly into the features of her friend.

"Assist me now to dress my wounds," remarked the prophetess, "and change my garments, then I will tell you all."

That night—the first after the great battle of the causeway, the Spaniards occupied the inclosure, surrounded by the wall, in which were the secret apartments; and, during the long, lonely hours of the night, Tonatiuh and Mazina watched and listened to hear the approaching footsteps of Maxtla or the strange priest, but daylight dawned, without their having heard the welcome tread.

* * * * * *

Nearly eleven months passed by after the defeat of the Spaniards on the fatal causeway—at the period of evacuating the capital; what a change had taken place during that time! Out of the little band of disarmed and disheartened soldiers, who survived that fearful slaughter, sprang up, almost by miracle, a large and formidable army, which marched again to the capital, headed by the immortal Cortez.

How this was accomplished, was a wonder, and it is most probable that no head, save Cortez, could have consummated so magnificent a triumph. At first he had been reduced almost to starvation. He and his little remnant of followers were compelled to kill and devour the flesh of their horses; but, gradually, he advanced, step by step; gained a little here and a little there; obtained victories where certain defeat appeared inevitable; quelled riots, discord, and discontent; gained allies at every turn, until he again stood triumphant at the head of an army, far superior to that with which he had previously entered the capital.

He had caused thirteen vessels of different sizes to be built, and they were tried on the waters of Zahuapan—a river of Tlascala. Then, they were taken to pieces, and the timber, anchors, iron-work, sails, and cordage, were placed upon the shoulders of *tamanes*, or porters, and, in this manner, conveyed over steep eminences, rough mountain passes, and through deep forests, to Tezcuco lake.

With such indomitable perseverance as this, and determination of purpose, as fixed as the stars in the heavens, who wonders at his success? Not one day out of the eleven months was he idle. His whole soul, might, mind, and strength, were centered upon this one point—the subjugation of the nation; and to this end, every resource of his genius was brought into play.

Thus, at the end of one month less than a year, we find him back, hanging as a dark pall around the capital, with his forces so arranged as to command every avenue leading to the city. His brigantines had been launched, manned, armed, and were already masters of the lake; thereby placing the capital in a close state of blockade.

During this lapse of time, there was no change in the Aztec monarchy. Cuitlahua, Montezuma's brother, after a short reign of four months, died with the small-pox.* He was succeeded by *Quauhtemotzin*, or Guatemozin, as he was called by the Spaniards.

This prince was young, yet amply experienced in military matters. He was not long in making himself perfectly acquainted with all the movements of the invaders. He had spies in every section of the country, sought allies of all nations, buried the hatchet of discord and enmity with disaffected tribes, and soon gathered around him a legion of warriors, formidable and desperate.

He commenced immediate preparations to meet the Spaniards; sent from the capital all useless members of the population, called around him all the potent vassals from the surrounding country, heaped up stores of provisions against the day of need, and sought by every means to strengthen the defences of the city. He reviewed the troops daily, excited them to deeds of desperation by wild harangues, encouraged his people to attack the white man wherever he could be found, and offered a price upon every Spanish head.

This was the state of affairs in the capital, when Cortez set his stakes for a siege.

* "This fatal epidemic was imported into the country by a negro slave in Narvaez's fleet. It first broke out in Cempoalla, and swept with fearful destruction over the country, smiting down prince and peasant, and adding another to the long train of woes that followed the march of the white man."

CHAPTER XX

THE GLORY OF THE "HALLS OF MONTEZUMA" DEPARTS—THE REVELATIONS AFTER THE CONQUEST—CONCLUSION.

Cortez had so stationed his army, as to hold full command of all the causeways, while his brigantines cut off communication by the lake. He had, also, dispatched a company to the hill of Chapultepec, to destroy the aqueduct which supplied the city with water.* Thus dispersed, he commenced active demonstrations by furious assaults upon the fated capital.

On the occasion of his first penetration into the suburbs of the city, he was agreeably surprised to find hovering around his person, the strange recruit of the fortress, who saved his life in several instances, during his previous sojourn in the capital. He also discovered the black robed priest, in whom, at that period, he became deeply interested.

If Cortez calculated upon a speedy termination of the war, by a surrender of the capital, he was greatly mistaken. He had yet to learn the indomitable courage, perseverance, and determination of the Aztecs, when led by a brave, shrewd, and able commander. Cortez was not, however, content to remain idle, and wait the tedious process of reducing the city by starvation and thirst; he was continually penetrating into the suburbs, carrying with him death and devastation. In these sorties, he engaged the populace in battle, burned their houses, and laid waste the capital.

After a weary struggle of months, through all kinds of fortune, whose record reads like the siege of Troy, the memorable morning of August 13th, 1521, finally dawned upon the smoking, pestering, starving capital. It was the day of slaughter, and the day of triumph. Cortez had followed up

---

* The water in lake Tezcuco, by which the capital was surrounded, was quite salt, and unfit for use. All water for drinking, or domestic purposes was brought to the city, through large earthen pipes, from the hill of Chapultepec,—some two and a half miles distant.

his advantage, until he had laid in ruins nearly all the city—until heaps of Aztecs lay piled up in every street; on every *azotea* where their bodies exposed to the scorching rays of the sun, created a stench almost insufferable,—until the besieged were reduced to the most painful extremes.

In all this strife—through all those fearful scenes, the strange Aztec recruit (who, it will be remembered, shot old Lord Ahuitzol) and priest, stood resolutely by the side of the Spaniards. They had performed mighty deeds of valor—had won laurels of renown, not only in the estimation of Cortez, but of all who witnessed their bravery and their deeds. They had received many wounds, but still fought on—courting danger everywhere.

At this period of the siege, Cortez drew off his troops, and made an effort to persuade the young, brave Guatemozin, to surrender, and save the lives of his subjects.

"Guatemozin would die where he was," was the laconic reply, "but he will hold no interview with the Spaniards."

How deep rooted must have been their hatred toward the treacherous invaders, to have induced such a reply. It was worthy of the man and his people.

The proud Aztecs were conquered. Through slaughter which stains the memory of Cortez with blood, the race were made to wade:—men, women, and children alike, were cut down; and Guatemozin was, at length, a prisoner. Cortez commanded him to his presence. As Guatemozin approached, Cortez advanced, and received him with a frank open courtesy.

"I have done all that I could, to defend myself, and my people," the prince said. "I am now reduced to this state. You will deal with me as you wish."

Cortez was filled with admiration at the courage and noble bearing of his royal captive, and assured him, that he should be treated with all honor. He dispatched an escort to conduct the royal family to the *azotea*. The escort soon returned, accompanied by the royal household, among whom was Mazina.

The scene which followed, was one of deep interest. It was the moment of the Spaniards' triumph in the new world, and the downfall of the Aztec empire,—such a moment as only comes at intervals of centuries.

Guatemozin begged that the massacre might be stopped, his subjects provided with food, and allowed to leave the infected city. This was readily granted, when the unhappy monarch, with his family and friends, sat down to the sumptuous banquet prepared for the occasion.

At this moment, the man in black robe and mask, who had excited such personal interest in the mind of Cortez, stepped from the ranks. He raised the black cowl from his head.

"General Cortez!"

Cortez started. Before him was *a man of his own country!* His thick, black beard and mustache were carefully trimmed; and there was an expression in his countenance, which puzzled the Spanish general, who gazed fixedly into his face.

"Who are you?" asked Cortez.

"Your own cousin," replied the uncowled priest.

"Luis?" gasped the general.

"Ay, the same!"

"Great God! how did you come here? We thought you dead!" exclaimed Cortez, with intense feeling.

"Nearly twenty-two years ago," he answered, and his eyes were moistened with tears, "a Spanish ship was wrecked on the eastern coast of this country. It was a terrific storm, and appeared as if heaven and earth, with the mighty deep, had conspired to render the scene memorable. On that ship were many souls, who, for days had been drifting before the tornado. Among them were two brothers—young men—and their wives. They each had a darling child,—one a girl, and the other a boy, both being about the same age—a little less than a year old." The man paused, wiped his eyes with the sleeve of his bloody robe, then proceeded:—"When the wreck came in sight of the rocky coast, all hope of escape was abandoned. The wind still blew a hurricane, the sea was lashed into fury, and the ship tossed like a drunken thing. On she went toward the breakers, rushing furiously upon the rocks. She struck broadside, bounded away like a frightened gull, and trembled upon the crest of the receding wave; then, on she came again, stern foremost. This time, there was a tremor, a rush, and the ship went to pieces. I was standing upon the prow of the ship, when she struck, and held one of the little children, the girl, in my arms; while its mother clung to my waist to prevent being swept away by the waves, which were constantly breaking over us. The shock threw us far out into the boiling surge. I held to the child, and clung to the weeping mother; but, she was torn from my grasp, and I lost sight of her forever," Again he paused, wiped his eyes as before, and appeared deeply affected. Every one present were so entirely absorbed in the narrative, as to take no notice of what was passing around. The man continued:—"When I arose to the surface of the water, the ship had disappeared, and not a soul was in sight! That instant, a huge wave passed over me; and, as it rolled on, I saw the form of the little boy, a few feet beneath the surface. I eagerly dove down, caught hold of his garments, and brought him up out of the water. While struggling to retain them both and reach the shore, a mighty avalanche of water came rolling on, raised me and my burdens high upon its trembling summit, and, with one hurl, carried us far up on the rocks. I was severely bruised, but had managed to protect the children. As soon as I could recover, I rose to my feet, and gazed around in hopes of discovering some other one of the unfortunate crew, who had escaped. I could see nothing but bits of the wreck, floating on the waves, and, along the shore, huge piles of rocks, extending as far as the eye could reach. When I was fully satisfied that the children and myself, were the only survivors of that fearful wreck, I took the little ones in my arms, and ascended the mountain. As I reached the summit, I discovered several Indians, far down in the vale. They did not discover us, and when they had passed on out of sight, I descended into the valley. It was impressed on my mind that we should be killed if we remained white, as we were. So I found some berries, undressed the children, and stained their bodies with the juice, which gave them a dark, tan color. I then buried in the earth, all their clothes except a small cloth placed about their loins; the climate being hot, they were not uncomfortable. This accomplished, I disrobed myself, and went through with the same process. Reserving only my pants, I buried the rest with the children's. In this manner I proceeded boldly into the country, and was not long in finding inhabitants. They manifested considerable surprise at finding us but we were treated kindly, our complexion being so near their own, doubtless saved our lives. We were brought immediately to this great city, and here sold as slaves. Fortune, however, so far favored me, that I never lost sight of the children. The boy was sold to a stone-cutter, named Ytzcoatl, and, when old enough, learned the trade, from which he arose to freedom and renown. The girl was sold to a noble; and, as she grew, her beauty developed, until she attracted the attention of Montezuma, who caused her to be adopted. Her situation was therefore changed from slave to daughter, and the master to guardian. I was sold as a slave in the temple, but, eventually, succeeded in becoming one of its priests, in which position I have been, nominally, for over fifteen years, and during all that time, I have watched over the interests of those children —Maxtla and Mazina—with a father's care. I was instrumental in bringing them together, in causing an affection to spring up in their hearts, which has bound them together forever. I ——"

He was interrupted by the strange recruit, who stepped forward, gazed steadily into his features, and exclaimed:

"Don Luis de Velasco!"

The words were winged with pathos. Cortez sprang to his feet.

The priest trembled from head to foot. Suddenly, and as by magic, the outer garments fell from the recruit, revealing the ample folds of a long, gay, and rich robe, sparkling with jewels, precious stones, and gold. He then threw off a tight-fitting cap, which had concealed much of his features, brushed back the heavy mass of his dark hair, which fell in confused disorder upon his shoulders, when the fair, full, and symmetrical form of Tonatiuh the prophetess, was presented to their astonished gaze.

Mazina sprang forward, threw her arms around the woman's neck, and wept aloud.

"O mother!" she sobbed; "I thought that you were dead! It has been so long since I have seen or heard of you."

Tonatiuh led Mazina to the priest, and inquired:

"Is this young lady, the person you saved from that wreck?" and her voice trembled with suppressed emotions.

"It is!" he replied. His keen, black eyes were fixed searchingly upon her.

"And you are her father?" Tonatiuh continued; her voice scarce above a whisper.

"Yes! she is my own daughter," he answered mechanically, not appearing fully to comprehend the astounding transformations which were passing before his eyes.

One moment, Mazina was folded in the woman's arms—a burning kiss pressed upon her cheek; she then reached out her hand toward the priest, and, in broken accents, sobbed:

"Luis! have you forgotten Dona Sonora?"

"Dona Sonora!" gasped the man. "She was my wife!"

"Dear husband! and I am her!"

"Sonora! My long-lost wife!" and he caught hold of her arm; while he gazed into her face, as if he would scan her very soul.

"Did you place this locket on Mazina's neck?"

"I did!" he replied.

"Was it not your wife's portrait?"

"It was!"

"Did she not have your miniature?"

"She did!"

"Is that it?" and she removed from beneath her robe, a large gold locket, and presented it to him.

He eagerly opened the locket, gazed first upon the picture, then upon the woman. His eyes filled with tears, and his arms clasped around his long-lost wife and child.

There was not a dry eye upon that *azotea*. That reunion after an elapse of more than twenty years, and under such peculiar circumstances, was a scene widely differet from that to which they had been accustomed during the past four months of siege, of famine, of blood, and of death. At that moment, a figure, covered with dust, blood, and wounds, crawled upon the *azotea*, and came feebly forward toward the group. Mazina, breaking from the embrace of her father and mother, flew across the area, and was clasped in the arms of Maxtla Ytzcoatl. A slim youth, with long, flowing hair, approached close to the group around the table.

Maxtla was led forward, and an explanation made of what had been developed, during which he manifested considerable surprise, but warmly greeted his uncle and aunt, and again clasped Mazina to his heart.

Then there was a slight movement, when Toluca—again mysteriously brought into light and life, as if by the power of the evil one—having ascended to the *azotea*, rushed upon the lovers with frantic desperation, and would have dispatched them both in an instant, had not the youth sprang forward, and, with one stroke of his cutlass, completely severed the right arm of the villain, causing his uplifted weapon to fall harmless on the floor.

"Fool!" hissed the youth, dropping the point of his sword. "You shall not triumph. *Meztli has been revenged!*"

He threw off his disguise, and there stood Meztli, her face full of scorn for her victim, while she smiled as she beheld Maxtla and Mazina folded in each other's arms. The cowled priest that was, but now Don Luis de Velasco, turned to Guatemozin, who had been deeply moved during the scenes, and reminded him, that if he had his disguise of the "white haired stranger," the scene would be complete.

The prince acknowledged that he was the person who had often befriended the lovers in that disguise, stating that he first used it, in order that he might pass unknown among the subjects of his illustrious uncle, and learn the state of feeling entertained by the populace toward their sovereign.

When the facts of Toluca's conduct were made known to Cortez, the villain was conducted from the *azotea*, and shot.

Cortez then proposed that Maxtla and Mazina should be married, as a crowning act in the scene. Mazina blushingly consented, when the Spanish general ordered Father Olmedo, the army chaplain, to perform the ceremony. Their names, as given at the bridal, were Sonora de Velasco, and Alouzo de Costa.

* * * * * *

Ten years rolled on, and the great capital had been renovated, rebuilt, and was now the head-quarters of the Viceroyalty in New Spain. During that time, Don Luis de Velasco, with his recovered wife and daughter, accompanied by her husband and Meztli, had made a long visit in Spain, and returned again to the valley, around which were associated so many recollections of the past.

They located themselves for a permanent residence, in the beautiful city of Iztapalapan, from which they could overlook the capital, and far across the valley was visible the wall, in which were located the secret chambers, and to which place they made frequent visits.

They owned a large palace and lived happily together, and many were the times that Don Luis de Velasco was importuned to relate his adventures, while with the Aztecs. Here Sonora his wife, no longer Tonatiuh the prophetess, would sit hours together, and relate to her little grandchildren, the particulars of her own trials, from the time she found herself lying in a nook of rocks, after the great wreck, down to the moment of finding her husband and child, whom she had so long mourned for as dead.

Here, Mazina—who was still called by that name, and Alonzo de Costa—Maxtla, the sculptor, passed many, many happy days; and here, also, was Meztli,—the strange child of the Aztecs. She was faithful to her pledge, given to Alonzo when he rescued her from the "cages" under the *teocalli;* yet he had more to be grateful for than she, and the kind-hearted Aztec was far from being a slave in the family of her friends. She was a dear and cherished companion, and Mazina's children called her "Aunt Mezzi," for many a year of blissful association.

Meztli's revenge was consummated in the great glory of the house of the Slave Sculptor!

THE END.

www.ingramcontent.com/pod-product-compliance
Lightning Source LLC
Chambersburg PA
CBHW031346160426
43196CB00007B/750

*9 7 8 3 7 4 4 7 9 6 2 1 7 *